Peter Lewis was born in the forty-fourth y premiership drought. He was educated a Boys' High and later attended Sydney Uni studied Arts and Law and edited *Honi Soit*

Peter has worked as a news journalist for *Australian Associated Press* and the *Daily Telegraph* and is currently employed as a media adviser to NSW Attorney General Jeff Shaw.

He is married, lives in Marrickville and named his cat after Mario Fenech.

the Convert

A Fan's Journey from League to AFL

Peter Lewis

IRONBARK
Pan Macmillan Australia

First published 1997 in Ironbark by Pan Macmillan Australia Pty Limited.
St Martins Tower, 31 Market Street, Sydney

National Library of Australia
cataloguing-in-publication data:

Lewis, Peter, 1966– .
The convert : A Fan's Journey from League to AFL.

ISBN 0 330 35997 5.

1. Sydney Swans. 2. Australian football teams—New South Wales—Sydney. I. Title.

796.336099441

Typeset in sabon 12/14.5 by Midland Typesetters
Printed in Australia by McPherson's Printing Group

Contents

Foreword

For most of my life there has been little appreciation, on either side, of one code of football by the other. Rugby league (and union) was labelled 'grunt, groan and grope' by the Mexicans, and Aussie Rules a girl's game, signposted as 'aerial ping-pong' by the lads from the northern states. Over the last decade television has helped break down the barriers, but the largest contributor to Sydneysiders (in particular) learning Aussie Rules has been the Swan's recent great year, aided by the war in rugby league.

The Convert catches the dilemma of the rugby league fan, while at the same time entertaining and informing us, as Peter Lewis learns about the code of AFL; it's rules, vagaries and history. This 'outsider' actually sees the scene in Sydney a lot clearer than many old Aussie Rules fans.

Peter's game-by-game journey and journal is a great description of an unbelievably exciting season. I can attest to this thrill factor because, for the first time since I was sixteen, I was able (courtesy of Channel 7 and 3AW) to go to the Swan's games without playing, coaching or commentating. It was just fabulous.

The Convert diverts slightly from the AFL when Peter talks about Wally Lewis and the rugby league State of Origin, that great showcase of the rival code. He explains the anti-Queensland feeling and inadvertently reveals why the two-state rugby league clash is a heaven-sent Hollywood script sports duel.

Peter also learns about our men in white who are always right when it goes the Swan's way—I mean that's really knowing your footy! I was pleased when he cottoned on to the attractiveness of the game as a spectacle, but I got lost when he talked about the mullet haircut! You can really sense the two cultures at work when Peter interviews local NSW players like skipper Paul Kelly and emerging ruck star Greg Stafford.

The Convert

The pace and spectacular nature of the game of AFL is matched by the narrative of *The Convert*. The end result is a terrific read—one which will be a very welcome edition to the library of any fan from any football code. And while I'm on that point, let us remember that Australia is the only country in the world that has four codes of football all doing pretty well.

Ron Barassi

Preface

This book came into being when Plugger booted a point from 60 metres on a heady night in mid-September. I had pitched the idea of a story of a rugby league fan's conversion to Aussie Rules at the start of the 1996 season and the reply had been: 'Good idea, but who's going to be interested?'. By early September, the Swans were the Sydney sports story of the year and I tried my luck again. 'If they make the grand final, the book's on,' was the reply. So when the Great Man, totally numb from the waist down, lined up for the shot that took the Swans from obscurity to an MCG play-off for the Premiership, I had more riding on it than most.

When the ball soared through for that vital point, I realised I had a major job on my hands—to do justice to the Swans' incredible story. In the following pages I've tried to translate some of the passion that I developed for the game during the 1996 season. I've tried to give newcomers like myself a broad overview of the game's rules, history, personalities and future. But before I'm cut down in flames from long-term students of the game for my presumption, I would like to point out a few things that this book does not aspire to. It is not definitive, it is not authoritative, quite often it's not even right. It is not an academic work and it does not claim to have particular inside knowledge. I claim full ownership of all errors and omission, but make no apology for them. Myths and half-truths are the stuff of all sporting 'knowledge'.

If anything, this book is 'The Outside Story of the 1996 Season'; the year from the outer, as just one of the thousands of Sydneysiders who flocked to the SCG tried to get a handle on this weird celebration of Australia. The purported facts and theories are based on personal observation, pub conversations—even a bit of genuine research. I would particularly pay tribute to Kevin Taylor's excellent history of the Sydney Swans which was an invaluable resource. I also consulted Mike Colman's definitive recount of the Super League war, *Super League: The Inside Story*. As a new fan, I would also pay tribute to Gerard Wright's coverage of the game in the sports pages of the *Sydney Morning Herald* where he successfully introduced Sydney to its footy team in a series of imaginative profiles and match reports. And like all true Swans fans, I choose to read *Footyzine* for a macro view of the game.

My main resource in preparing this book, however, has been people; people who have given their time to share their thoughts about the game with me. I would particularly thank three fellow travellers who made the ultimate sacrifice and allowed me to turn them into literary characters: Justin Lucas, Eddie Greenamy and Eddie Witalec. These are the guys who nursed me through my first Swans season and put up with all the stupid questions. They also offered invaluable assistance in the revision of this book. Thanks also Sid 'The Clock' Marris, Anthony Sharwood, and Edwina Throsby for contributing their prose; Jason Harty for the Swans' profiles; Meredith Burgmann, Bob Reynolds, Helen Meyer and Ange Collins for their input into the fans' profiles and Sydney Swans' media manager Steve Brassell for his assistance in organising interviews with the players. Thanks also to Karen Adams for helping transcribe the interviews and Ian Heads and Pan Macmillan for giving the project the green light.

The following people also offered their words of wisdom at various stages: Dave Page from *Rugby League Week*; Griz and Anna, Iain Johnstone, Craig Davis, Kenny Brandon, Tony Dass and Braham Dabscheck. Special thanks to the Boy Genius and Sandy for braving my hangover and putting me up in Melbourne over grand final weekend. My heartfelt thanks also to my wife Ann for tolerating my decision to extend the footy season by three months with such good humour.

Finally, I can only dedicate this book to one group of people and they are the Sydney Swans; a team that gave a city which had lost its sport to a corporate war a new reason to look forward to the weekend. Without their sensational performances, the gutsy comebacks which became the hallmark of 1996, this book would never have been written. Without them, there would be no Sydney converts to write for.

Waiting for the
Bounce

Death of League

I would never have picked myself as a Swans fan.

I grew up in the shadow of the fig tree at Bear Park, a devoted fan of North Sydney, rugby league's least successful team. I attended school across the road and cheered my heroes bleak winter after bleak winter.

The Bears were perennial losers—even their rare victories were tainted by the certainty of future defeat. But I loved their incompetence and never-say-win attitude. Their mediocrity spanned the 1970s with players history quickly forgot: Mal McLachlan (my first hero), Paul Hope, Neville Makin and Aub le Broq. I collected their footy cards and cajoled them for autographs as I sat on the Miller Street wall watching them blow another half-time lead. I cried myself to sleep the summer that half the Bears signed en masse with the hated Manly Warringah.

In the 1980s they flirted with success, signing a brace of Kiwi internationals (Mark Graham, Olsen Filipania, Clayton Friend and Fred Ah Koiu) and a rugby star (Mitchell Cox). Under successful coaches like Tommy Bishop, Ron Willey and Frank Stanton they promised much, delivering little but heartache. I traversed my teens rejoicing at the odd victory against the hated Manly and urging the Bears home as the Avco Angels attempted the rumba.

They made the semis in 1983 and lost both games convincingly. The rest of the decade was spent with or around the wooden spoon as coaches quit mid-season and any player with a future signed with a more successful club at the first opportunity. Throughout these dark years, we loyal dreamers would meet on the pavement in front of Percy's, the pub across the road from North Sydney Oval, for a pre-game beer, strolling expectantly to the dry ground just before kick-off—there were never queues to deal with. We'd trudge back to Percy's at half-time and stay there if things were going badly. If the Bears were still in the match we would wait till full time to drown our sorrows.

A renaissance in the 1990s gave me the thrill of semis at the Stadium. In 1991 and again in 1994, the slick and professional Citibank Bears won knockout games to put themselves into grand final play-offs. Both years they shied at the final hurdle. In 1991 Daryl Halligan, the king of goal-kickers, missed a match-winning kick from in front. In 1994 the Bears tackling machine, Garry Larson, had a brain explosion. Norths' Mr Clean got sent off for a spear tackle minutes after we had secured a match-winning advantage when a Canberra Raider had been dubiously marched. On both occasions, the elusive grand final appearance was inches away, but the Bears were denied. As we primal screamed our despair in the back of the Bat and Ball Hotel we took solace in the certainty that the first flag since 1922 was surely close at hand.

The modern fusion of skill and incompetence, success and failure, that tantalised me in my youth was still irresistible. I would follow the Bears until they secured the inevitable title. Then I would reap the fruits of those decades of failure, I would hail the Mighty Bears as the Premiers marched down Miller Street, allowing a generation to finally die in peace. I was a fan for life, uninterested in other diversions; I was a Bear man and that was my sole perversion.

Then there was a war. One of those grubby corporate wars where there are no good guys and everyone gets caught in the cross-fire.

And, hard as it is to believe with the benefit of hindsight, no-one saw it coming.

These were rugby league's salad days. John Quayle, a one-time international forward who went straight from the paddock into sports administration, and Ken Arthurson, the long-time Manly powerbroker, had hauled the game out of the morass of mediocrity, violence and corruption which threatened to kill it in the early 1980s. The pair had transformed the League, expanding the Sydney competition to Canberra, Brisbane and other regional centres, broadening its appeal to women by cracking down on dirty play, even making inroads in the southern states.

The 1994 season saw some great footy. Even though the Bears missed the grand final, you had to admire the skills of the all-star Canberra side. The Green Machine absolutely munched Canterbury to win the title. League was glitz and glamour, Tina Turner and the Men of League calendars, packed stadiums and kids dreaming of growing up to be Kangaroos. The Australian tour to Great Britain that year was the icing on the cake; three epic Test matches played with State of Origin intensity, showing the British were narrowing the skills gap with Australia and making League a genuinely international game.

But beneath the surface, cracks were appearing. Expansion clubs like Brisbane and Canberra were dominating the competition, benefiting from their one-team town status. With a captive market for sponsors and large junior areas, the clubs had a natural competitive advantage over the

Sydney teams. The Brisbane Broncos, the League's first privately run club, had excelled through the early 1990s both on and off the field, winning back-to-back titles and running things like a modern business. Meanwhile, the foundation inner-city clubs were struggling for exactly the same reasons; contracting junior branches, extra competition for sponsors, not enough talent to go around. As the balance of power shifted, the expansion clubs were demanding a greater say in the running of the game. A principal gripe was the uneven competition, that some clubs were no longer competitive and should be cut.

The League had attempted to impose a level playing field in 1990, instituting a player draft and salary cap. The draft, used in most other football codes including the AFL and NFL, gave the worst performing clubs first choice of players the following season. The idea was to constantly equalise the talent at each team's disposal. But a 1991 Industrial Court ruling that the draft amounted to a restraint of trade killed off the redistribution of wealth initiative and the League was left with a salary cap that was widely abused by the wealthy clubs.

To compound the League's problems, Quayle and Arko decided to sit on a 1989 report recommending a cut to the number of city teams. The report mounted a compelling case for the need to raise standards by developing an elite competition, with a handful of 'super clubs' in Sydney, and an increasing number of expansion teams. But the administrators, most of whom had loyalties to the same clubs they were being told to exterminate, ignored the advice. The League had thrived under Arthurson and Quayle because they had made good business decisions, but at the vital moment they acted with their hearts over their heads. Instead of contracting, the League decided to establish four new clubs in 1995, taking the Premiership to a twenty-team comp stretching from Perth to Townsville to Auckland.

just to sign on the dotted line. Even mediocre reserve graders were walking away with $40,000 in the hand. The ARL wanted quantity, enough players to disable Super League.

The bidding peaked with both camps courting Kangaroos half-back Ricky Stuart. Caught between a goldmine and a vault of cash, Stuart let slip the quote that, for me, embodied the Super League war. Asked which competition he would join he replied (with a straight face) 'Ricky Stuart has to decide what's best for Ricky Stuart'. For many thousands of rugby league fans, battlers who worked hard and loved their footy, the game was already dead.

When the dust had settled, the player resources were split pretty evenly between the warring corporations. ARL had the bulk of the players and twelve clubs. Super League had eight existing clubs, most of the stellar names and significantly, the governing bodies in Great Britain, New Zealand, Papua New Guinea and France—effectively the rest of the League-playing world.

The war went into the courts: ARL attempting to enforce the Kerry Packer-induced loyalty agreements, News Ltd arguing such contracts were in breach of Trade Practices legislation because hey, this is a business, and we can do whatever we like.

The 1995 season ground on against the backdrop of the Federal Court case. Super League clubs and players became openly hostile to the ARL, their attacks gleefully chronicled by the Murdoch dailies. The ARL responded by overlooking all Super League stars for the State of Origin series, despite a court order that they should be considered. They were considered, was the offical line, but the ARL said it was looking to the future of the game. Thus, the Australian captain Laurie Daley missed out while newcomers like Gold Coast's Ben Ikin got a gig. The season ended in an-ARL loyal Manly versus Super League-convert Canterbury grand final on a sombre September afternoon where acrimony and distrust overshadowed all the qualities that had once made the game great.

As the rival camps prepared to establish separate competitions in 1996, I, like many other fans, took stock of the situation. You couldn't blame the players; some were just kids who had never asked to be custodians of an eighty-year tradition caught in a power play between two corporate giants. I didn't blame them, but I couldn't imagine myself cheering for them either.

Days before the two competitions were scheduled to begin, Justice Burchett delivered the ARL a stunning and comprehensive victory. In the Federal Court Super League lawyers attempted to side-step the decision while its players vowed to sit out the season. But when the Judge handed down a no-pay, no-play edict, Super League 1996 collapsed.

Within days lawyer friends were telling me how atrocious the ruling was, how Burchett had delivered an emotional ruling, how News Ltd would surely win the appeal, how this was not the ARL's victory, only its stay of execution.

Disillusioned and disgusted I left my city office. 'League is dead,' I said to myself. 'The Bears will never be the same.'

I wandered through the streets of Surry Hills, up towards Moore Park. There was nothing premeditated, just a walk to clear my head. I started thinking about how the world was changing and I shouldn't try to hold it back. I should be adopting an expansion team for myself, a team I knew would be around long enough to give me a return for my passion. But not League, which now seemed poisoned by its own avarice. I needed a new sport with no emotional baggage.

I thought of the Sydney Swans and how they'd struggled to gain acceptance in Sydney since they relocated from South Melbourne more than a decade ago. I had always related, albeit from a distance, to their lack of success and was clearly impressed by their record losing runs over the early

'90s. On a whim, I wandered into the Swans office and bought a member's ticket.

I'd offer them a season and see what we did for each other.

First
Quarter

Them's the Rules

These are the rules of the game as far as I have gleaned after one season.

⟨ The team that scores the most points win.

⟨ A team gets six points for kicking the ball between the two big posts.

⟨ A team gets one point if it kicks the ball between a big post and a small post; if it hits a big post; or if the defending team touches the ball before it goes through any post. If the ball hits the small post, too bad. The opposition gets a free kick.

⟨ Possession is always up for grabs when the ball is moving. Players can kick or handball the ball to a team-mate or bounce the ball and keep running themselves.

⟨ If a player catches a kick on the full, it's a mark. He can stop and have a free kick or keep on running. If he goes for the free kick, the defender takes his spot on the mark where the ball was caught.

⊘ Players can be tackled between the shoulders and waist. If the defender goes higher or lower he concedes a free kick (never a 'penalty').

⊘ If a player tries to run with the ball and is tackled, he concedes a free for 'holding the ball'. If he doesn't get a chance to move, the umpire calls for the ball to bounce. The rule leads to the most contentious of calls in tight play: has the player tried to run? If the crowd think he has they'll call 'BAALLLL'. (They'll probably call it anyway.)

⊘ If the ball goes over the boundary line, the umpire throws it back in over his head and shoulders; if it's kicked out on the full it's a free kick to the other side.

⊘ If a player commits a particularly vicious infringement or makes a smart comment to the umpire, he'll be marched 50 metres upfield. This is the 50 metre penalty.

⊘ Off-side is a foreign concept and shepherds are totally legitimate.

⊘ There are no sending-offs, players can be reported for striking after the match and face suspension if found guilty.

⊘ The only other rule is that there are no other rules as far as I can tell.

First Impressions

Sunday, early April, the Sydney Cricket Ground. As a kid I came here with my father to watch Test matches, Lillee and the Chappells my larger than life heroes. I drank beers with my underage mates on the Hill at day-nighters in the days before the grass was covered with plastic chairs. I was there when Newtown lost the 1982 grand final to Parramatta, perched on aluminium cans in a vain attempt to see the action. The SCG had always embodied the magic of sport for me. The contests would flash past your eyes, as if you were the witness to a crime. Then they'd be replayed on television, somehow more valid when they had been broadcast than in the flesh. Finally, years later, you'd see the scenes in archival films; they had become part of sporting history, the only history you had ever witnessed first hand.

The SCG was adopted by the Swans as their home when they made the move to Sydney, presumably because it was the largest oval in town. Rules is a game of wide open spaces, not the 10 by 100 metre grid. The grounds down south cover hectares; by national standards the SCG is a pokey little quarter acre plot, yet it was as good as central Sydney could offer. Over the years the small ground has come to serve the Swans well; while visiting teams got cramped and disoriented bumping into each other, the Swans weave around, flaunting their intimate knowledge of the turf like a well-drilled marching band.

This first Sunday, about 10,000 punters show; stretched out around the plastic seating they resemble strangers in an airport departure lounge. The opposition is Fremantle. The Dockers were the second team brought into the AFL from the West, part of the expansion of the Victorian League in the late '80s and early '90s. Unlike Sydney, Western Australia was an Aussie Rules stronghold and it had been obvious that it could support two teams. The Dockers were known for their visually challenging purple and green uniforms and their running play straight up the centre of the ground.

The Swans had gone to Adelaide for the first game of the season and had been annihilated by 90 points. Armed with new coach Rodney Eade, and an improved showing in the second half of 1995 which saw them scale the dizzy heights to twelfth spot, the Swans had been expecting better. But the news from Adelaide was grim. Disorganised defence had let the Crows in for 20 soft goals, while Sydney failed to get the ball anywhere near their most potent attacking weapon, star full forward Tony Lockett. After fielding just three kicks in the first-quarter, 'Plugger' ended up in the ruck. The Swans won more ball with him there, but had no-one on the forward line to kick goals.

Sympathetic commentators suggested Sydney was just getting used to Eade's new style of play. Unkinder souls suggested it was an opportunity for Eade to get used to Sydney.

So here I sit at the SCG, ready for my first game, open-minded but just a tad underwhelmed. The early highlight is the access to the Noble Stand my members pass gave me. For someone who had grown up dreaming of SCG membership from the Hill and old Sheridan Stand, this was

16

luxury, an opportunity to watch the game from the bar. Call me easily impressed, but I was.

Ten minutes before the bounce (that's kick-off) the teams make their entrance through giant crepe paper banners. The huge signs are memorable for their dubious artwork and corny messages, normally focusing on one of the players celebrating a milestone (Derek will Kick-it today!) or offering a hokey little ode to battle. The players start their warm-ups, a routine comprising of a half-paced jog, the old sideways skip and a few practice kicks. Then the one minute warning siren sounds and the teams spread out into position.

It strikes me how little I know about the game.

This is what I do know: You get six points for kicking the ball through the big posts and one point if you kick the ball between the big post and one of the little ones. If you catch the ball on the full you get a mark and if you run too far you have to bounce it. If you want to pass the ball to a team-mate you have to punch it. The referees bounce the ball in the centre and throw it over their shoulders from the boundary line. And that's about it.

Luckily I find a seat next to Eddie, an old Newtown iden-tity, who I'd never picked as a Swans fan. He coaches me through the opening exchange, starting with the ground rules. 'The first thing to remember is it isn't the referee you bag,' he says. 'The Bamfords are called umpires, when you're not calling them "white maggots".'

'The second thing is you don't call for a penalty, it's a free kick or just a free.'

Linguistics settled, play begins. Once the ball is moving the field is awash with action. The game had always appeared restricted, compartmentalised, disjointed on the television; the cameras skipping from kicker to receiver. In the flesh it's smooth and fluid.

Too smooth. The Dockers start with a flurry, all speed through the hands. In contrast the Swans look like they have stage-fright, continually baulking as if trying to remember their lines. A Swans defender kicks the ball straight into the arms of a Fremantle player and the Dockers have kicked a goal before they've worked up a sweat.

To me, it looks like thirty-six players run in random patterns, but Eddie assures me there's method to the madness.

'What you've got to understand is that Aussie Rules is about the only ball sport where there's no off-side law,' Eddie explains. 'In soccer, rugby, League, American football, you name it; the players are constrained by the off-side rule. They're given limited access to the arena. In Rules there is none, any player can run anywhere they like on the field.'

'So how come they look like they know what they're doing?' I ask.

'You basically have different lines of attack across the field,' he tells me. 'See Plugger?'

'He's the only one I know.'

'Well, he's a full forward, that's the main attacking line, like your centre-forward in soccer or designated hitter in baseball. The seagull, the glory-boy, the show-pony. His job is to break free of his defender and mark within kicking range. The best of them can kick ten goals in a game—and Lockett's the best of the best.

'Around the top of the goal circle is the half-forward line; that blond guy is Craig O'Brien—he used to play with Plugger at St Kilda, can kick a goal too. Then there's the centre line which is—guess where?—and behind that the half-back and back lines. Usually the coach will allocate three players to each line.'

'So it's like attacking zones?'

'Sort of, the players have basic areas to patrol but there's lots of movement across the park. Defenders will leave their zones to pick up a free player further downfield. See how Paul Roos is holding the ball now?'

18

'Why's everyone boo-ing him?'

'That's not a boo, it's ROOOOOOOOOS. He's a legend, played nearly 300 games, came to Sydney from Fitzroy two years ago. Safe as houses and looks a treat in his thigh-guards. He's holding up play to allow some of his followers to get into attacking positions.'

'I thought the followers were in the grandstands.'

'I forgot to tell you, there are three extra players, not listed in the set positions. A tall bloke to contest the rucks, and two quick guys who are expected to be on the ball all day—they call them ruck-rovers and Paul Kelly, that little bloke who looks like a rat, is as good as they come. He won last year's Brownlow—the AFL's best and fairest award.'

True to Eddie's analysis, Kelly bursts through the centre scramble and sprints downfield towards the Noble Stand. A surge of excitement builds as the ball floats towards the posts. Tony Lockett, looking twice the size of his two opponents, starts moving towards the ball, almost in slow motion. He leaps skywards, hands spread and swallows the ball just beneath the posts. 'PLUGAAAAAAAAA' we scream, the call catching in a euphoric gurgle at the back of the throat.

'So how come he's walking back from where he caught it?' I ask.

'Where you catch the ball is the mark. That's where the defender can stand. The marker can kick from anywhere behind that point, provided it's in a direct line with the goal. Sometimes the ump will stop them running around the mark when it's a tight angle.'

'White maggots!' I offered, chancing my arm with the lingo.

'Exactly. And there's another thing about marks you should know. Just because you take one doesn't mean you have to stop and go back to play it. You always have the option of playing on. Only thing is, if you start to play on and run off the mark, you can't change your mind—a bit like life really.'

Plugger kicks the ball between the big posts assuredly and a roar goes up around the ground as the goal umpire rocks back on his heels and signals six points, giving the SCG its first opportunity of the year to cry: 'How big is it?'

As the game progresses, I begin to get a feel for the play. League is a lateral and linear game, vertical runs and horizontal passes dominate. The field is grided up and even the players look like boxes. In contrast, Rules is circular, the players constantly moving in waves, almost circles, around their designated section of the field. Attackers search for open space, while defenders try to collar them. Sometimes the defence will double team a dangerous player, leaving another attacker free elsewhere on the field. It becomes a race to get the ball to the free player. Then the ball stops moving and the crowd cries 'BALL'.

'What's that?' I ask.

Cursing the ref, er, umpire, Eddie fills me in. 'Holding the ball; it's got to be the least understood rule in the game. If a player tries to run with the ball and then gets tackled, it's a free kick to the other side for holding the ball. The whole idea of the game is to keep the ball moving and if you can't, you're penalised.

'But if the player gets tackled before he gets a chance to move, that's OK. The umpire balls it up and the play starts again. All the controversy lies in the interpretation, did the attacker have time to move? Basically, whenever anyone gets caught in possession it's worth a shout.'

'Like calling for a second-row feed at the League.'

'Yeah, except the umpires occasionally award one for holding the ball.'

Sydney looks good in patches, moving the ball downfield quickly into the zone where Plugger lurks. But whenever the ball gets near him, the final kick goes awry or Lockett is so heavily marked he can't get through to meet it.

'This game is all about getting a free player in attack and then getting the ball to him. Sounds simple, but the execution is everything,' Eddie says.

That's what's happening. Both sides have their share of possession, but it's the Dockers that convert. In the second quarter Fremantle kicks five straight goals. It's not that they're all over the Swans, it's just their attacks end in goals, while Sydney's finish with a spilled mark or an intercept across the forward line.

Still, trailing by just five points at half-time, the Swans are holding their own and the closeness of the scores adds to the excitement.

A Fremantle Docker goes low, executing a perfect grass-cutting tackle. The crowd erupts in howls of protest and the umpire awards a free against him.

'What was wrong with that?'

'You can only tackle between the shoulders and the hips,' Eddie explains. 'Any higher is too high, any lower too low.'

'Why?' I'm bewildered that the one skill I built my rugby career around is outlawed in my new game.

'Beats me. Them's the rules.'

That's what following a new code of footy is all about, accepting the rules, trying to understand them, not trying to find an underlying logic; just knowing the appropriate time to abuse the umpire.

Another free kick is awarded against the Swans, this time for a tackle going too high.

'This has to be the most contentious of all the rules,' Eddie tells me. 'Basically you can wrap up a player around the shoulders, but you can't come in over the shoulder. The test is the direction of the defender's impact. You can reach up, but not come in with a downwards motion.'

My brain is beginning to get bogged down by the detail.

'For a game that looks like a mad scramble there's an awful lot of rules.'

'Ah, but there's a saving grace. All these rules for high and low tackles only apply when you are on the ball. Sure there's a general melee rule that prohibits fighting, but if you're away from the action it's basically anything goes. See Dunkley and that Fremantle forward wrestling on the ground? No problems—they're just "jockeying for position".

'And there's another thing. No sending off. If a player does go the cheap shot, the worst they'll do is get reported to the AFL tribunal and face suspension the following week. This means two things: one, you don't get games ruined because some whistle-happy Bamford sends your star player off for a love pat. And secondly, sending a hitman out specifically to disable an opposing player is a viable match tactic.

'You see, Rules is a pragmatic game; there's a lot of the Irish in it. If you think of rugby union with its excruciatingly technical rules as the natural product of the English culture, you can see Aussie Rules as its absolute antithesis. The rules are limited to ensuring players don't get maimed but anything else is worth a try.

'And if you want proof of this theory, I give you the knee in the back rule, the ultimate fifty cents each way technicality. Basically, it's illegal to use an opposing player's back as a launching pad for a mark. You are not allowed to go the big leap. You can't set your knees in your marker's shoulder to soar high for the ball. But there's one exception. If you successfully catch it, everything's OK; the fair mark overrides the foul and you're a hero rather than a thug.

'The rule is pure pragmatism. The player must sum up whether he's going to mark the ball or not before launching into the leap, knowing the stakes are high either way. Essentially, the rule prohibits reckless stupidity unless it is executed to perfection. If you can grasp this concept, you'll understand the game.'

The Swans are battling on, exhibiting more than their quota of reckless stupidity. But I find myself more interested in the supporters than the players' uneven attempts to claw their way back into the game.

Rules crowds barrack with a different intensity, the excitement surges rather than peaks. The crowd constantly involved rather than merely interested bystanders. I have developed a theory about this: it all comes back to the different rhythms of the two games.

League is an arm-wrestle, six up, six back, kicks for position, no mistakes, possession is all. One side attacks, the other defends. A typical game may end up four tries to three, that's seven times in eighty minutes when a team achieves its ultimate goal. That's when the crowd explodes. If the try comes from a bomb or a burrow from dummy half, so be it—it might not look pretty, but it's success.

The infrequency of these major scores dictates the rhythm of the game. To keep the juices flowing, League fans focus on infringements. In ascending order of excitement: technical fouls such as off-side ('been doing it all day ref'); fumbles which surrender possession to the opposing side; and, at the top of the fulcrum, acts of violence, such as head-high tackles or the piece de résistance, an all-in brawl. That excitement is compounded if your team benefits from the infringement through a kick at goal or the sin-binning or sending off of an opposing player. In this way it is the referee whose rulings often generate the major moments of a game of League.

In contrast, a game of Rules offers scores of scores. The six-pointers, the behinds, the near misses. Marks by the minute, constant challenges for possession, ball movement across the park. Of course, the goals send the crowd into a frenzy, the fans behind the big sticks providing the impetus for the rest of the ground, creating a Mexican sound wave as they jump out of their seats to celebrate. But the frequency of other highlights produces its own crowd dynamic. Indeed, every play is a contest for possession. There are cheers as marks are plucked, possessions gained, defenders shrugged off. The passions of the crowd will ebb and flow until a player gets caught and the cry of 'Ball' goes up. Then there is a bounce and it all starts again.

The cheers dissipate into groans as the Swans fail to peg the Dockers. But as the Swans stagger, we in the stands don't fall silent. Instead, we try to give them a bit more to work with. There is something about the cheering at a game of Rules, a manic edge foreign to a League fan. League is a game of control: control of possession in attack, control of the attacking side in defence. Aussie Rules is more random, notoriously unpredictable. At any moment fate can play its hand, as the bounce of the little red Sherrin dictates possession. Every second of every game, possession is up for grabs, a stark contrast to the certainty of League's six-tackle rule. And when the going is tough, when your side needs that little bit of luck, there's that delicious possibility that the cheers of the loyal fans may just tip the ball your team's way.

But even this theory and the cheers of 10,000 Sydneysiders can't bridge the gap and when the final siren sounds, the Dockers have run out 29 point winners. The result was never really in doubt. Sydney tried hard, throwing everything at the Westerners, but when it mattered the ball would fall short of the mark. A Docker would intercept or the kick for goal would go wide. There was no problem with the enthusiasm but a big question mark hung over the finesse.

As we file out of the ground the chilling realisation hits me: I may have discarded one lost cause, once source of heartache and agitation, for another.

Positions for Beginners

FULL-BACK: The last line of defence, the full-back and back pockets are responsible for blocking out the opposing side's full forwards and getting his own team's attack moving. As Melbourne's Paul Bulluss discovered at the SCG, the beaten full-back can be very exposed and look very silly. Job requirements include a true boot, the ability to judge when to mark and when to punch, and calmness under pressure.

HALF-BACKS: While the League backline is made up of the pretty boys with a sidestep and hairdo, the AFL half-back line is the home of the unsung heroes. These are the guys who get the ball out of trouble and up to the mid-field. The best of them are never isolated, using the kick and the pass to get out of trouble. Are referred to as centre half-backs and half-back flankers.

WING: The quick men who can set a game alight if they get some room in the middle. The most likely players to go the lope and bounce the ball upfield, also tend to be the most likely to go too far and surrender possession. For every Stuey Maxfield blitz along the wing there's half a dozen that go nowhere. Like their League colleagues, can rarely be trusted in defence.

CENTRES: The real tacticians of the game, responsible for positioning the attack with long, raking kicks or short, sharp hand passes. They control the square, the point where all attacks become threatening and all defences feel the pressure, marshalling the followers and coordinating the rest.

RUCKMAN: The tall beanpole who would play in the second row in rugby union and sit on the bench in League. The main players at the bounce and throw-in, their job is to get the initial touch of the ball and propel it towards their rovers. The best of the ruckmen will also turn up on the half-forward line to kick the odd goal and in defence to win a possession. Not noted for their speed.

ROVERS: As the half-back calls the shots in League, the rovers mould the attack in Rules. Only they scrounge and kick and scratch for possessions as well, rather than waiting for the ball with their hands on their hips. The rovers are expected to be everywhere, just off the ball at every contest and injecting themselves through the pack to threaten the goals. Paul Kelly has set the benchmark as the tough little rover.

HALF-FORWARDS: The half-forwards lead a schizophrenic existence, responsible for delivering quality opportunities for their forwards while always keeping the option of their own tilts at goal open. When the half-forward line is working it is a second focus of attack, drawing defenders away from the forward line to give the full-forwards space. Also play an important defensive role in preventing full-field attacking waves.

FULL-FORWARD: The true aristocrats of Aussie Rules. They may not rack up a high number of possessions but the full-forwards and forward pockets work for their chances. Stand behind the goals and watch Plugger in action, the ball may be just starting its way down the other end but he baulks and weaves constantly, trying to make a break and time a run to coincide with its arrival. The full-forward goes for the vital marks and if successful must kick the goals. All the guts and all the glory.

Fan Profile

Eddie Greenaway

Eddie Greenaway the converter. With partner Angela Collins he is one of Australian football's disciples, spreading the gospel through Sydney's inner suburbs. A long-time editor of 'zines'—the ultimate in public access publishing—Eddie has been producing the cult underground zine Eddie *for the past five years. In 1996 Eddie, togther with Angela and Dianne Buckley, embarked upon a new venture and released the first two issues of* Footyzine, *an anarchic collection of fans' reminiscences, anecdotes and dubious theories of football and life—how ironic that the first such fanzine dedicated to Australian Rules was produced in Sydney. Eddie can be caught any match day in the bottom deck of the Noble Stand.*

I've always supported a red and white team, since I was growing up in north-western Victoria and backed the Robinvale Eagles in the Sunraysia competition. Then I moved to South Australia and it was the North Adelaide Roosters, another red and white mob, who I supported until I moved to Sin City.

I started supporting the Swans to get behind the code. In the early 1990s they were a laughing stock and it had got to the stage where there was serious talk of wrapping them up. So we decided we should go along and start supporting them'.

A few years ago we had a comp that everyone associated with *Eddie* magazine played in, so that sort of got us into the game. So it started as support for the code and in the end you also support the team, because you're turning up each week and who else are you going to barrack for?

There's a lot of humour in watching footy. It's not just aggro, it's a party. I think the more you go, the more you get into it and the less you actually drink. When you first start going to the games you end up getting really pissed. But as you get more engrossed in the games you just don't want to cloud the experience. The true addicts are those who don't drink anything until after the match.

Footyzine arose out of interest generated by the Sports Issue of *Eddie* magazine. That in itself, was a pretty revolutionary thing to do—an underground look at sport. At that stage it was an absolute no-no to mention footy or any kind of sport in the trendy inner-city. Serial killers had more street creed. You had your art scene and your pub scene and your music scene, but we uncovered a latent sport scene as well.

We were also motivated from going down to Melbourne and seeing some of the amazing football exhibitions they have down there, like 'Eyes on the Ball'. It just makes you aware of how football lends itself to art, yet it's something the mainstream media doesn't look at, at all. Anyone from anywhere has festivals and cultural outpourings, ethnic based or whatever. What Melbourne has is football. It's unique, it transcends boundaries, it just strikes a communal chord.

The Sydney fans really changed this year after the Geelong game. There was an influx of people who didn't really understand what was happening. The attitude was slightly different too, almost like at the opera, people there for the spectacle, holding their mobiles, asking who the players are. If you started barracking hard, as you know we do, they'd either give you a strange look or move. We're not into obscenities, it's just very passionate barracking, but I don't think it's something rugby league crowds are used to.

One of my most memorable games of 1996 was against St Kilda. We drove down to Melbourne in the Swanmobile and then out to Waverley Park, which is way out in the south-eastern suburbs. It was the coldest day of the year and they call it 'Siberia' there anyway. We were buying beanies and scarves and anything we could get our hands on—the old ladies selling old South Melbourne gear outside the ground were doing good business.

There were probably about 5,000 Swans fans and the St Kilda fans were going off—hating the Swans because they'd bought Lockett and O'Brien. The guy behind us got so angry he was dropping his trousers and waving his willy at Plugger. We weren't that surprised, St Kilda fans have a reputation for being pretty feral.

The reaction to the Swans in Victoria has always been schizophrenic. On the one hand there is a soft spot because they've always been easy beats and were originally a Victorian-based team who were also easy beats. Take Fitzroy and St Kilda, for example, and you see that losing teams quite often have a good deal of secondary support. The Swans are a lot of Melbourne people's second team, especially people whose favourite team has struggled. They're extremely one-eyed, they hate every other Melbourne team. That's where the Swans fit in quite well—they're not from

Melbourne and, up until 1996, they were always losers.

However, the more successful the Swans got the more the Victorian media will play into the alleged Sydney–Melbourne rivalry. There's also a sort of snobbery about supporters down there—that if you haven't barracked for a team for fifty years you're not really a proper fan. So they probably think all Sydney's new fans have sort of cheated.

The massive resurgence in old Swans fans coming back to the fold is very exciting and, if the club maintains a healthy attitude towards the old South Melbourne base, then we could have the best of both worlds—a successful future and a rich history, a history which more new fans should learn. Personally, I'd like to see the Swans wear the old white jumper with the red V for games in Melbourne, so there's that extra connection for old South fans. But we'll have to see what direction the corporate Swans machine decides to go!

The pressure I see for the Swans long-term is if it continues to win, the big money from Sydney business will start rolling in and it will be like there's this shiny, new team and no-one will be interested in the unsuccessful parts of it. So I'm a bit worried about the Swans growing without an appreciation of their history, their tradition as a losing side, which is something intrinsic to the Swans.

I hope the team consolidates in the top four for the next half dozen years and maybe wins a flag. But also just to stay up there and be a team that kids want to play for. If they do, there'll be more kids playing Rules in the parks and when that happens, Sydney will have really made it.

A Flying Swan

Same place seven days later, back in the bottom deck of the MA Noble Stand. There are more people this week, reflecting Collingwood's superior Sydney support base to the Dockers. Collingwood, I learn, is the most loathed of the AFL clubs; the Magpies' ugh-booted, duffle-coated supporters, borderline dirty tactics and long-term success have earned them universal dislike amongst other teams. This isn't a Manly-Warringah, Silvertail, chip-on-the-shoulder type of loathing, but a simple case of recoil at lowlife.

After ending their longest-ever losing streak last year, Sydney knocked Collingwood out of the semi-finals in the last game of 1995, Plugger farewelling outgoing coach Ron Barrassi with seven goals. But the pundits all predicted a Pies win today—not able to go past the 27 goals they kicked the previous week, Sydney's dismal form in the first two rounds and the fact that two of the Swans' pivotal players, Paul Roos and Mark Bayes, are on the injured list.

Out in the centre, the game is held up while LA honey-rap couldabeens, Kultcha, give an especially nauseating a capella version of the national anthem. I think I know why some singers like Julie Anthony, Johnny Farnham and the ironically named Kultcha regularly accept the football anthem gigs. Belt out 'Advance Australia Fair' and patriotism compels the audience to stand up, stop talking and actually listen to you.

But after fifteen minutes of play we're wishing Kultcha had given us all three verses plus the anthems of all other member nations of the UN. The Magpies are up four goals to one before our stomachs have settled. Saverio Rocca, the Pies' star full-forward and big brother of Swans new recruit Anthony, kicks the first and the big black and white banners are waving under the Southern goalposts. We get a cheer when Lockett threads the ball through the posts from near the boundary line after shrugging off two Collingwood markers with a zagging run to mark. But a succession of five straight free kicks puts Collingwood on a roll, a 50 metre penalty from the ruck leading to a simple shot.

There is already a resigned acceptance amongst the old heads in the Noble stand. Three losses out of three. They'd been through it for so many seasons and 1996 looks like being another long winter.

What gets me, though, is that it doesn't stop them cheering like maniacs. When Sydney takes a mark, you could have kidded yourself they were playing in the grand final on the MCG.

'The secret with following a losing team,' Eddie confides, 'is looking for the positives.

'Take that tall guy out there, Greg Stafford. He's as close to a ruckman as we're going to get this year. Born and bred Sydney boy, grew up next door to Wests' home ground. Now he's playing in the AFL.

'The scoreboard mightn't look too flash but I reckon "the Golden Staff" is holding his own against Monkhurst. And that, my friend, is a little victory.'

Rising to Eddie's analysis, Stafford grabs the ball in the centre square and sends a beautiful 60 metre torpedo punt kick straight into Plugger's clutches. We zero in on the big man and watch the ball pierce the posts and land a few rows in front of us.

From the restart it's Stafford again, marking over the back of a Pies defender, the sort of leap you see in the news highlight packages.

'He's been around a few years now, Stafford,' Eddie continues, warming to his commentary. 'Played a few senior games last year but he was never reliable; like a lot of gangly guys he was all arms and legs, no co-ordination. But I make the bold prediction that Greg Stafford will have a huge year for the Swans.'

With that rave review, Stafford sends a woeful kick towards goal, straight into the Collingwood man on the mark and the Magpies bolt away.

Then another first: O'Brien competes with a Collingwood defender near the boundary line. They leap and both miss the ball, but the Magpie's elbow lands right on O'Brien's head as he returns to terra firma. Play is held up as the Swan forward is stretchered off, blood coming from his ear.

I'd always accepted the Sydney stereotype that Rules was a softer game than League, devoid of the intensity of the six-tackle rule, the head-high tackles, knees in the back, the Christmas holds. But over the course of the season I would find new respect for the aerial ping-pong boys. When they get hit, they stay hit. When they collide, they do so at full speed. Often it's a case of two players heading in opposite directions at full speed, their paths converging without either realising it, leading to a blind hit. Other times it's a gutsy rover like Kelly, all hands and head, scrambling for the loose ball amongst the boots. Or the bloke on the ground who cops the sliding knees or boots from a desperate defender. And these are the legitimate injuries, the cases of bad luck in fair play. When a player actually decides to play dirty, going the swinging arm at the head of a player who is trying to mark the ball, there is even greater capacity for serious injury.

While O'Brien tries to remember his name, another Swans player puts up his hand and introduces himself to the 17,000 at the ground. Number 27 has been scrambling around the ball all game, picking up a few possessions in the centre of the ground. Now he runs across the top of the goal circle to mark a misdirected kick intended for Lockett. He steps in deliberately from 35 metres, sending a beautiful kick high and long through the goals.

'Who's that?' I ask, feeling like I do when I sit in on an episode of *Melrose Place*.

'Wade Chapman.' I'm informed. 'Another teenager we picked up in the draft a couple of years ago. Wouldn't recognise the improvement after a couple of years under Barass.'

Barass, of course, is Ron Barassi. The tough-talking coach and motivator extraordinaire who took on Sydney at its lowest ebb and coached the team through 1993, '94 and '95, years that all long-time fans only mention in hushed tones. While he had decided to step aside this season, Barassi was still a presence behind the scenes, where he would watch in satisfaction as the group of kids he'd moulded together, matured like fine wines.

He's smiling now too, as Sydney is back to within one goal after its sluggish start. The Swans launch another attack straight up the centre of the ground, through a lanky blond guy who is identified as Troy Luff, running the ball out of the back line and setting up Plugger for his third goal.

'Luffy's been in and out of firsts for years,' Eddie says. 'Each season he looks like being cut and each year he just survives.'

Lockett steadies in front of the posts.

As with all great athletes, he follows a strict and methodical routine when preparing to kick for goal: pulling up his left sock, then his right sock, a deliberative snap of the underpants out of the cleft with thumb and forefinger, before lowering his head over the ball and pacing deliberately in. As usual, it works and Sydney has hit the lead.

Despite a second goal to Rocca just before the siren, Sydney is giving its supporters a game and we rise to cheer the players off at quarter time. They have come back from being three goals down to trail by just four points.

'This is promising,' Eddie bubbles. 'They're playing the perfect game for the SCG, straight up the centre, rather than stuffing around on the flanks where play can get congested on such a small ground. I may be wrong, but after fourteen years' practice they just might be getting the hang of it!'

The second quarter is minutes old when Chapman kicks his second. Collingwood replies immediately but the Swans have most of the attack. Two blond guys start dominating in the centre, numbers 11 and 39.

'What's the story with the numbers?' I ask.

'Each team picks a squad of 42 for the year and allocates each player a number. Generally you have a number for your entire career with a club. So the guys with 30s on their back aren't out of the under-23s or anything; it's just the luck of the draw.

'That number 39 is Adam Hueskes. They picked him up from South Australia in the draft a couple of years ago. He has a beautiful kick on him; has the odd brain explosion, but 90 per cent of the time he's rock solid.

'The other guy is Stuart Maxfield, he transferred from Richmond this year. He is the type of player we really need, quick down the flanks, with a long boot on him.'

And they're the skills Maxfield is displaying today; swooping on the loose ball near the centre square, sprinting clear of the defenders, invariably bouncing the ball and continuing downfield before zeroing in on the forward line. The first few times he sends the ball goalwards, Lockett lunges but just misses. On the third attempt, Lockett stretches back to reach for the mark, getting free of the Collingwood defender; but as the ball reaches him the dirty Pie goes the swinging arm across his face. The umpire awards a free, Plugger goes through his socks-and-snap routine again and it's Sydney by seven points.

Two other players stand out, both dark-skinned and skilful. The younger one is Michael O'Loughlin, a lanky kid who runs with his socks down. You can see his ability in the way he controls the bouncing ball—almost as though it's on a lead; what to many is a scramble for possession is an elegantly executed roping-in mission for him. Playing across the half-back and half-forward lines, he wins the 50–50 possessions that dictate the results of many games. The other is Derek Kickett, an Afro-haired, barrel-chested journeyman, blessed with the most supporter-friendly surname in the League. Aged somewhere in his mid-thirties, I'm told the crowds love Derek because he can do that little bit extra, those things which set him out from the pack.

'Like what?' I inquire.

'I'm not buying into any racial stereotypes here,' Eddie parries, 'but the very best Aboriginal players seem to have an extra sense on the football field. It's like they can see the spaces appearing downfield before they've actually appeared. Watch the way he kicks straight over his shoulder, how did he know Lewis was free?'

Sure enough, Kickett has picked out the fuzzy-haired number 3, Dale Lewis, who calmly converts from 40 metres.

'You also see it with the loose ball,' Eddie continues as the crowd erupts to applaud the 12-point lead. 'Derek just has it on a string, total control even if he's only one of a dozen pairs of hands groping for the ball. If you were a betting man, you'd put a lazy Lucky Lobster on Derek to get the ball every time.'

Right on the half-time siren Lockett kicks his sixth goal of the afternoon, grabbing the ball near the boundary, turning and snapping truly. Sydney goes to the break with a 17-point lead. We drink beer, eat hot dogs and talk of victory as the kiddies run out for the half-time entertainment.

Within a minute of the second half Sydney is out to 23 points. Lockett lunges at another mark but the ball clears him rolling towards the posts. Paul Kelly sprints onto the ball and almost runs it into the open goals, like a League three-quarter in the clear, before drilling it through with feeling.

'Hold onto your hats, but I think we've got a run-on developing here,' Eddie whispers.

'Say what?'

'When one team gets on top, the game can blow out. Whether it's superior skill, speed or commitment, they start getting to each contest for possession first. When that happens across the ground for a sustained period the scoreboard can start moving very fast indeed.'

And so I sit back and enjoy my first run-on. Sydney starts dominating across the paddock, movements leading directly, at times inevitably, to the goalposts beneath the MA Noble. Out of defence the ball goes to Maxfield who tears through the centre before picking out Lockett right in front of the posts. The big man again steadies and finesses the ball through, something almost dainty about the manner in which he caresses the little ball, like those cartoons of the gorilla patting the mouse.

Then big Stafford intercepts near halfway, soaring in front of a Collingwood defender, and finds Lewis deep in attack. Closely marked, he handballs to Kelly, breaks free of his defender and receives the ball back from his skipper, ambling around the sideline to goal from a sharp angle. Collingwood replies after intercepting a wobbly Andrew Dunkley restart, but straight from the ball-up Lewis swoops and punts the ball 70 metres to a surging Lockett. The big fella misses for once, but the Swans are back on the attack.

The run-on is captivating, the smooth precision of the movements so perfect to look at, like a painting hanging in a gallery. Only this is performance art.

Kickett is collared 80 metres out from goal and is given a free. He finds his captain in open space around to the right of the posts. Kelly kicks a sweet six-pointer from the acute angle. O'Loughlin gives Plugger the chance for number eight, after a beautiful dummy. The big fella surprises no-one by shooting accurately from 20 metres. The siren sounds for three-quarter time and Sydney is up by 35.

The turnaround has been fast and ferocious. If it were not for the five behinds in the quarter (a special mention here for Anthony Rocca) Sydney would be annihilating the Pies, who themselves have kicked three behinds for every goal since their four-straight opening.

Free of tension, the Swans fans start enjoying themselves, cheering the team home as it goes through the motions in the last stanza. The Swans only put on one goal, Kelly kicking his third after another Maxfield break, and six behinds: but it's enough to saunter to a 34-point win.

The players looked relieved rather than jubilant as they wander off the field. A lone spectator jumps the fence and sprints across the ground to the cheers of the crowd as the security men give chase.

'Bastards,' the regulars mutter. 'In any other ground in Australia you're allowed on the field for a boot after the game. Not the SCG. Instead you get a bunch of Hulk Hogan impersonators chasing you off.'

The howls of discontent, though, are drowned out as the faithful sing the Swans song. It's the first time I've heard this strange half-durge, half-ditty, but it's catching enough. Especially the bit about 'shaking down the thunder from the sky'. I'll have to remember to ask someone what that means.

What Club is That?

Collingwood: Universally despised inner-eastern Melbourne club, supporters wear duffle coats and ugh boots and spit at opposing players.

Carlton: The hated Blues. One-time battlers, but everything except Kernahan's Mullet has now been renovated.

Essendon: Home of Melbourne's second airport, isolated and ignored by the rest of the city.

Geelong: The Illawarra Steelers of Aussie Rules. Bleak industrial climate means football's the most exotic thing in town.

North Melbourne: Dying breed who inhabit dreary suburban wasteland. The only place in Australia that Wayne Carey would be regarded as classy.

Melbourne: Silvertail also-rans who are bankrolled by the Establishment. If it wasn't for the MCG members, they'd have none.

St Kilda: Perennial losers who gave Sydney Lockett and O'Brien. Supporters' passion only overshadowed by their anti-social behaviour.

West Coast: The 'Wiggles', successful expansion team who exude that WA Inc slickness and artifice. Not to be trusted with investment portfolios and small children.

Fremantle: Full of arty types who think Perth is crass; play an open game to match. Always beat Swans.

Adelaide: Chardonnay-sipping yobbos. Poor away-from-home form proof that Crows can't fly.

Brisbane: Like the Broncos without Wally Lewis, the Brisbane Bears are made up of hometown legends who are non-entities in the rest of the country.

Hawthorn: One-time glamour team, now fighting to stave off mergers. Rejected marriage with Melbourne in 1996 but only a matter of time before the Hawks get hitched.

Fitzroy: Softest fans in the League. Brisbane bound after deciding it was better to stay the Lions than merge with Carey's mob. They've had the stench of death for years.

Footscray: *Romper Stomper* and *Spotswood* were set there, but there's nothing Hollywood about this place. Even the grannies have Mullets.

Richmond: Collingwood fans with a yellow streak.

Captain Kelly

Paul Kelly is the soul of the Swans. The captain who runs after the ball all day, taking on two, three defenders and running away from the ruck contests with the ball. He's been doing it for years, right through those dark times when Sydney couldn't win a game. Only difference is that now he's recognised for his efforts, winner of the 1995 Brownlow medal and 1996 captain of the All-Australians. All this from a kid who used to mark a young Laurie Daley at five-eighth in the Juniors.

You're a bit of a convert yourself, having played junior League in Wagga. How long did you play it for?

League was my number one sport for years. I started when I was six and played right up until I was fifteen.

Wagga was Mortimer territory.

Yeah, the Mortimers, Sterling, Brentnall all those blokes. I was an Eastern Suburbs man so Kevin Hastings was my legend.

How did you make the decision to switch codes?

Every school in Wagga played every code so you got to play all of them. When I was about twelve or thirteen I actually went and had one year of Aussie Rules. I still played League in the afternoons, but I played Rules in the morning. Then when I was in under-15s I was playing League for Wagga Brothers and I either had to go from under-15s to under-17s or change clubs to play under-16s, so I thought 'I'll go and have a couple of years of Rules and see what happens'.

Were you a half-back in League?

Five-eighth actually. I used to play against Laurie Daley, he was from Junee and they were in our comp. His team, which also had Jason Lidden in it and a couple of Laurie's cousins—they were a gun side—they won every grand final from under-7s to under-15s.

How did you compare against Daley at that stage?

He was better than what I would have been. Sometimes I did all right against him, sometimes I didn't. Everyone knew he was going to be a sensation. I was only fairly small; I didn't really grow until I was sixteen or seventeen.

So was it just having to change League teams that got you into Rules?

Yeah, there was no big career move or anything; I was just a kid who wanted to go and play something else for a while.

Did you immediately fall in love with the game?

No, I was just playing footy. I obviously enjoyed it at school, where you went kick to kick and tried to take the speccies, but I was just enjoying it. It was something to do on the weekends.

And when did it get fair dinkum?

I really did enjoy the Rules and once I got started in under-16s, I just kept playing and got a bit better and a bit better and it all happened.

Did you play seniors down there?

Yeah, I played a year in the under-19s and then went into first grade for the Wagga Tigers.

What were the Tigers like?

We were pretty good. We got beaten in two grand finals when I was there. There were three teams in Wagga and clubs from the surrounding country towns like Griffith and Leeton. Daniel McPherson's team Ganmain-Grong-Grong-Matong was in the comp too.

Did you go to Sydney because Wagga was in their recruiting area?

At that stage, the Swans had the whole of NSW and they didn't have to draft or anything. If you looked like showing a bit, they'd put you on the list and that was it.

So how did it happen for you?

In about 1988 a couple of clubs started to show a bit of interest and the Swans got word of it, so they put me on the list and other clubs couldn't do anything. It was like they'd bagsed you.

Did you move straight up here?

No, they had a couple of train-on squads down there and I played a few of those games. I didn't really want to come to Sydney, I was doing my plumbing apprenticeship and I was just happy working and playing footy on the weekends. In 1989 they got me up for a couple of reserves games and then at the end of that year I finally moved up.

What was the change like?

I moved into a two-bedroom flat in Vaucluse, with a mate of mine from Coolamin who I used to play against. He'd been up here for twelve months. He got cut within the first two weeks I was here, so I spent the first six weeks by myself in this unit, no idea how to look after myself. It was a bloody nightmare.

Did you go straight into first grade?

I played the first game of the year in the Ones, against Carlton down at Princes Park. I played about ten seniors and ten reserves that year, so I was in and out a little bit.

How were the Swans performing then?

In 1990 we won seven or eight games and finished tenth or eleventh. That was when Williams and Healy, Toohey, Stevie Wright, Dennis Carroll, were still playing. So I'm glad I was there then because I got to meet all those blokes. We weren't too bad in 1991, then in 1992 it started to fall apart. We beat Brisbane at home in a night game in 1992 and then we didn't win another game until the end of 1993.

What was the football like during that streak?

It was tough going through it at that stage, but looking back now and going through the good times I can't believe how we kept backing up. It was shocking. We didn't have a good structure around the place either; we had no gym and no social club, no offices, we were stuck under a stand at the SCG, the off-field administration wasn't that good, the players weren't that good.

So that really translated to the performances on the field?

Exactly, we had no direction off the field and you could see it on the field.

What do you put the turnaround down to?

Probably Ronnie Joseph and Alan Schwab, who was with the AFL at the time, just before he died. They decided they were going to get Sydney to work. They got Ron Barassi and, importantly, the AFL's support. We got our own gym and our own social club and our own offices, a great board of directors, good office staff, it was just a huge turnaround off the field. And then you've got the right blokes picking the right players on the field. Rob Snowden had a big role in that. Ron Joseph got Tony Lockett up here. The combination of changes just made the club more attractive. Then at the end of 1995 we backed it up with Dyson, O'Brien and Maxfield, so there's been pretty good recruiting in the last few years.

Was there a bit more confidence before the 1996 season?

We knew we weren't a bad side, but we didn't realise that we were going to be as good as we were. In 1994 we could play three real good quarters of footy and lose it in one, whereas this year we could play three ordinary quarters and win it in one. That was the big turnaround.

It was like you could just push the button when you needed to.

Yeah. We could win games in a quarter, which is something that hadn't happened to us before.

How do you sum up the character of the Swans?

We're a pretty physical side and we never say die. We're in the game from go to woe. We showed this year where we had a couple of huge wins when we looked like we were down and out and we just came back and got over the line.

One thing that League fans always say about Aussie Rules is that it's a pretty soft game, but some of the hits are amazing. When you see an opponent get knocked senseless, do you pick them out and target them?

It's actually a bit hard in our game to line a bloke up because you can go any way. But you do get the occasions where you can get a bloke and he won't even know you're coming because you can hit them from any direction. That's where our game is a lot different from League. League's all up front and you know you're going to get tackled. But when you get hit and you're not ready for it, that's when you're really going to get hurt.

What's the most serious injury you've had?

I've had a reconstructed shoulder, hernias and knees and ankles—all that sort of thing.

Mainly from hits?

More wear and tear. We've got to train really hard and be really fit, so you just tend to get worn down over the years. I think the shoulder was a hit.

What is your role as captain? Do you fire them up before the big matches?

I'm not a big talker, we've got other blokes who are good at that. Paul Roos is great, and even some of the younger blokes like to say a lot. I don't rant and rave, I just go out there and toss the coin.

What about the tactics?

Well, the coach's making the moves from up the top of the stand, all the positional changes. In our game everyone is their own coach; you might have a bit of a captain on each line; Paul Roos might take care of his line, Dunkley his line, me with my line, Tony up the front. Because it's such a big ground it's pretty hard to take control all over, so it sort of works like that.

Everyone knows your name, especially after the 1995 Brownlow. Did that change things much for you?

I don't feel any more pressure. I actually think I had a better year this year playing footy than I did in 1995. Just a bit smarter and a bit older. I certainly got a lot more attention from other sides, but because the other guys were playing well, it just opened up more spaces for them. The publicity side of things has changed a bit in the past twelve months, more people notice you in the streets, but they're all well-wishers and that's great. The media are also pretty good up here, they sort of get on our side rather than wanting to put us down. In Tony's case the Melbourne press were always having a go at him and he had a real bad thing about the media, which was fair enough.

Do you feel like the Swans are becoming more a part of Sydney?

As a team? For sure. I think this year we would have been the most supported side of any sport in Sydney; sponsorship-wise and just in the numbers of people who wanted to come along to the games and watch us on TV. We were the number one side in Sydney and that's a pretty good feeling, coming from when they didn't really appreciate us to really loving us, it's a good turnaround.

Do you have a bit of a feeling of: you bastards, you've just jumped on the bandwagon?

Ah no. It's human nature, everyone loves a winner. Myself and all the boys are just enjoying the pleasure of having so many people coming along to the games and supporting us. It's good fun.

Before Plugger came up, who used to kick the goals for you?

Capper back in the late eighties, Simon Minton-Connell for three years, he kicked 50, 60 odd goals at full-forward. Jason Love kicked 40 or 50 a couple of years. But we never really had that dominating player up front.

Has having Lockett down there changed the way you play the game?

Pretty much, yeah. You set up your lines a bit differently. Some coaches like to handball the ball up. With others it's

49

just bang, get it down there fast. The Hawthorn game showed the different set-up, having the attack a bit further out.

Let's talk about early in the season. After losing those first two games were you thinking: this is going to be a long year?

It wasn't like that surprisingly. We'd been beaten by nearly 100 points, so you'd think it would be. But we'd had a pretty good pre-season and we knew we weren't going to be a bad side. But we were certainly disappointed with our performance. I don't know what happened, it was just one of those days and, remember, Adelaide did it to a few other sides after that. We weren't the only side to go over there and get whipped. They were just on fire at that stage and we came along at the wrong time. The Fremantle game— we just can't seem to get it together against them. They play a very different game—a keeping's off sort of style, but I can't explain why we can't play well against them. After that game, everyone else was pushing the panic button, the media had dropped off us, but there wasn't a great deal of panic in the camp. We knew we were going to be good enough and that it was just a matter of time before we settled down and had a win. Then we beat Collingwood and after that we had a pretty good run.

What about tactics in Aussie Rules—are you just all out there running after the ball or is there more to it?

There's a lot of tactics in it. But remember, the blokes from Melbourne can't work out what's happening in League either. It's a simple game to us, but to them it's hard to know what's going on. In Rules there are lots of different set-ups, if you've got a Tony Lockett you don't like to crowd him, you have the other blokes sitting out wider. You have different set-ups

But the growing pains of the Australian Rugby League were not the sole reason Super League evolved. The federal ALP Government had finally allowed pay television operators into Australia and the media giants smelled a financial windfall. Squeezed between lobbyists, the Government decided on a blueprint that would allow those who wished to operate the licences to fight it out in the marketplace. One of the media players who threw his cap in the ring was Rupert Murdoch. Originally exploring a consortium with Australia's other certifiable tycoon, Kerry Packer, Murdoch eventually went it alone under the Foxtel banner, adding it to his substantial media interests which included a major newspaper in every major city in Australia.

Murdoch knew the importance of sport to pay TV. To get people subscribing you need a product, something that people want to watch so bad that they'll fork out money for the privilege. In the USA it had been gridiron and basketball. In England, the Premier League soccer. Rugby league was an obvious parallel in Australia; a popular, television-friendly game with a loyal support base. The problem was that rival tycoon Kerry Packer had stitched up rugby league until the end of the century for the Nine Network after a rival network went bust in the recession. And so a bold alliance was formed between News Ltd, the corporate outsider, and a handful of clubs who considered themselves so far outside the ARL tent that they didn't mind pissing in.

Whispers of Super League surfaced in 1994, but it wasn't until February 1995 that there was anything in the public arena. Then, it was news that Super League was off; all twenty clubs had signed five-year loyalty agreements with the ARL after being read the riot act by Kerry Packer, who also snapped up the pay TV rights for good measure.

On April Fool's Day 1995, the game was turned on its head when Murdoch's daily newspapers revealed that eighty players, including leading internationals from Brisbane,

Canberra and Cronulla, had signed with Super League. The signings had been done in utmost secrecy, teams of players being ushered into obscure hotel rooms on the way home from games. The players were offered five figure sums to sign up, with the promise of six-figure contracts; there were bonuses for signing on the spot rather than getting legal advice, warnings that the offer would not be repeated. Like most blokes in their early twenties being offered financial security for life, they signed up. The Murdoch press characterised the raid as a religious conversion, as recruits spoke starry-eyed about their belief in 'the News Ltd vision'.

Seeing his television asset disappearing before his eyes, Packer mobilised. Ordering new right-hand man, and former ALP number-cruncher, Graham Richardson onto the case, a counter-attack was planned. The first move was to cash up, securing $100 million from Optus to neutralise Telecom's alliance with Foxtel. That Optus parted with the money showed there was an even bigger game being played. The pay TV lines which delivered the product into the subscribers' homes were the infrastructure upon which the information superhighway would be built. Whichever communications giant controlled the cables would have the upper hand when this even larger game truly kicked off in the early twenty-first century.

Against this backdrop, the ARL mounted a bidding war to secure sufficient players to neutralise Super League. While Murdoch had the big names, he hadn't snared enough middle-rung players to showcase his stars. The ARL's Phillip Street headquarters was dubbed 'the lolly shop' as players filed in to claim their lucrative contracts. The recruiting was overseen by Bob Fulton and Phil Gould, two high profile coaches who had the respect of many of the players. The ARL's tactic was to trump Super League by offering massive up-front payments and smaller long-term contract sums. Over a crazy fortnight, players were offered up to $450,000 at the throw-ins and the bounces, different players go to different spots.

So when you run out you basically know where you've got to stand at the set plays?

Yeah, but remember, you play more than one position during a match so it's not that simple, you've got to know where everyone's going. So you've got to be thinking out there, otherwise you get caught out. Some players get tagged too. I get a player following me every game and we'll have a player who does the same to other fellas. There are some players who you'd call positive players and others who are a little more negative, whose job it is to nullify an opponent.

Do you know the style of play other teams will come up with against you?

Sure. Most teams have a set style. Melbourne is a big handball side out the back. They'll get the ball and go bang straight out the back and they'll have two or three guys set up. Whereas, a North Melbourne, they'll get it and kick it straight to Carey. Adelaide is more a running side, while Fremantle keep it off you. So there are different styles of play.

Is there a particular style that Sydney is more suited to playing against?

I think we're pretty close to being one of the best sides in having least goals scored against us, so you could probably say we're a bit of a defensive side, so we like it pretty nitty-gritty and in tight.

What about the role of ruck-rover? What's its basic purpose? Is it like the half-back in League?

51

Yeah probably. Our job is to get the footy as much as we can and just run around everywhere.

I read somewhere you'd run about 18 kilometres in a game.

Yeah, probably. It's really up to yourself. You run around, then you can have a break on the half-forward flank, bring a bloke up, have a rest down there, play a spare man in defence sometimes. It all depends what sort of a tag you get. Some blokes can just run all day, so I'll go and have a spell in the forward pocket; I might come back and sit in their back half, just fill up space for their full-forward, it depends on the tactics you are playing.

One other thing I wanted to ask you about was the Origin series, what are they like?

I didn't play last year because I was injured. But I've played every other year I've been selected.

Did they work as a concept? The club matches are practically Origin anyway.

Yeah, that's a problem with our game. We put so much emphasis on club footy that we'd rather play for our club than our State. Whereas the League blokes are a bit different. While that's the case it's always going to be difficult to get a really good series and the people don't seem to support it anyway, a lot of the good players aren't there for one reason or another.

They all have injuries that time of year.

Yeah, something like that. But I love to play in it, if I could've played I would have.

Have you got any regrets, having started out as a League player, that there's no Australian side that goes and plays against other countries?

Yeah. This year I was named captain of the Australian side. But we can't play anyone. It would be a big thrill to run out leading your country onto the ground but you don't get the opportunity. That's the only really down side to Australian Rules, I reckon.

Finally, how do you hope Aussie Rules grows in Sydney?

I'd love to see the kids in the parks playing kick to kick with footy jumpers on. That's the one thing you don't see up here, or very little of it. We are starting to get the young kids involved, but that's got to be our focus.

Things That Go Bump
in the Night

There is a magic about sport at night. It might be the triumph of human endeavour which allows a massive arena to be lit in the first place—the giant light-towers erected at the SCG as part of the peace settlement in the World Series Cricket war are still a source of awe some fifteen years on. It could be the physical sensation of being part of a night crowd; feeling, smelling the heat of the battle against the cool night air. Or it might just be that stars shine brightest in the dark night sky, the dreams always more vivid against the black backdrop. Whatever your theory, it's impossible to deny that a sports event under lights has an extra allure. From my very young days watching in awe from the hill at Leichhardt Oval as the Bears made their only final since World War II (losing to Balmain in the 1976 Amco Cup final) the night game offered that extra bit of theatre.

The Swans have been allocated a handful of night games at home in their draw although it's difficult to see why there weren't more. The night games provide a greater sense of an event that is missing on a Sunday arvo. Where the day match is a relaxed adjunct to the weekend, the night game demands to be placed in the social diary—this is a weekend night after all. As with all night entries in the diary, this requires sacrifice and a serious build-up, including a meal beforehand and a range of pubs at which to meet the party. The night game fans are better fed, better dressed and better lubricated by the time they enter the ground. There is also the expectation of entertainment, not just a footy game but a piece of theatre, something worthy of an entry under 'Friday night'.

The taste for the magic is why thousands of Sydneysiders are making a beeline for Moore Park on a Friday night. It's the round six game against Essendon and the Bat and Ball is chock-full of suits wearing Swans scarves, the new look of the CBD; competing for drinks with well-dressed girls on their way to see Alanis Morrisette at the Hordern Pavilion next door. Both acts are riding high; Alanis thanks to saturation FM airplay; the Swannies because they've won three in a row, a feat regarded impossible just a month ago.

After the Collingwood win, Sydney travelled to Waverley Park, a massive concrete stadium on Melbourne's outskirts, to play Richmond. I was at one of those Sunday afternoon barbecues where everyone sits outside in the autumn sun and frowns on suggestions of televised sport. I'm forced to come up with a wide and increasingly tenuous range of excuses to leave the yard and make furtive trips upstairs to keep tabs on the Swans' progress. On the huge field the Swans are struggling. Each time I flick the box on, they seem further behind on the scoreboard.

By three-quarter time my trips up to the TV are becoming suspiciously regular and I give up all pretences, parking myself in front of the box for the final quarter. The Swans are 20 points behind as the minutes tick down, Kickett winning some vital balls to set up one, two, three Lockett goals. Suddenly, Sydney is a point ahead and the lounge-room is full; the same people who had raised an eyebrow at me before are now cheering without any self-consciousness. We hold our collective breath as the seconds tick down, captivated by our first real nail-biting finish, while Andrew Dunkley punches for the boundary line from a series of restarts, snuffing out the Tigers' last surge. When the siren sounds, we let out an unrestrained whoop for the Bloods' one point win and start taxing our limited footy knowledge with fatuous post mortems: 'They were always on top', 'They outmanoeuvred them in the final minutes', 'The Tigers lack a real finisher'—that sort of nonsense. Sydneysiders may not know much about the game, but it doesn't stop us spouting what little knowledge we possess as gospel truth.

The Swans had made it three straight wins the previous Saturday night, the season's first game under lights, edging out Hawthorn by two goals. Again the match was in the balance until the final ten minutes, when Sydney desperately defended a six-point lead. With every player, bar Lockett, in defence, the Swans crowded out the Hawks' last attacking surge. When Sydney booted a goal after the siren we nearly lifted the roof off the Noble stand as the Swans mobbed their star for the night, Craig O'Brien. It had been O'Brien's six goals from half-forward which had overshadowed the two big-name kickers: Lockett and Hawthorn's Jason Dunstall. All night, O'Brien coolly converted his chances, the bulk of the goals kicked from out near the fifty, while the star attackers struggled to get a look at the ball. His performance underlined the conviction that Sydney was no longer a one-man show, that teams which just concentrated on snuffing Plugger out might get hit from another angle.

So expectations are high as we head towards the beacons of the SCG, glowing through the cold drizzle which enveloped the city. A crowd in excess of 20,000—Sydney's largest for the season—has gathered for the spectacle and chatter expectantly, like first-night theatre patrons. Essendon is one of the AFL's glamour sides, whose red and black strip ensures they're this former Bears fan's second favourite team.

Sydney storm onto the field through the giant banner. They are led out by their leading men: Kelly, Lockett, Kickett and Roos. These are the personalities who give the Swans their primary identity: the rugged skipper, the giant goal machine, the midfield wizard, the consummate professional in defence. These are the recognisable faces, the stand-outs for the uneducated Sydney audience. These are the ones around whom the script will be written, who are vital to the pending drama, who set the themes that will underpin the plot. If you want to characterise the Sydney Swans go to these four men: guts, glory, brilliance and poise.

Of course, once the ball is moving anyone can bid to get into the act. First it's Shannon Grant, a compact, crew-cutted wisp drafted by Sydney two years earlier and still a teenager, who steps onto centre stage. The Swans boy-wonder delivers a perfect kick to Lockett—not a mark, but a perfectly weighted ball that bounces and lays up just so for the big man. Lockett handballs to the flying wingman, Stuart Maxfield, who bursts through two tackles before dropping the ball off the boot. There's no-one home in the Essendon goal as the ball bounces slowly towards the point stick, then takes a 90 degree turn to wobble through for the first goal.

Grant is one of those talents who pick up Best Supporting Actor Oscars; the ones who deliver the openings for the stars, whose job it is to make them look even better. With a long accurate boot and a magic pair of hands, Grant turns up anywhere from full-back to half-forward to spark an attack.

He's one of a group of Swans whose low profile belies their importance to the side. There's Brad Seymour, the square-jawed defender who is always in position, cleaning up the rubbish while Roos and Dunkley take the headlines.

Kevin Dyson, an ex-Melbourne star whose massive boot can link the full-back and forward line with just one transaction. Darren McPherson, a fresh-faced kid from a country team called Ganmain-Grong-Grong-Matong, and Peter Filandia, a pint-sized rover who used to play for the Bombers, cover the acres in defence, filling the huge spaces Kelly leaves as he sticks on Essendon dangerman James Hird like glue.

The thing about these guys is you won't cheer their name each time they get the ball. You probably won't even recognise them: hell, there's thirty-six blokes out there running in all directions and you're struggling to keep up with the ball. You don't notice the good things they do because they're not the knockout punches, the eye candy that newcomers to the code notice: the long-reefing goals of Plugger, or the 50 metre runs from captain Kelly. These are the guys whose job is altogether more intrinsic; they create the platform on which the show-stopping scenes are built.

Here's another supporting player, Daryn Cresswell, the sure-handed rover, working out of defence. I'm told Cresswell is a stalwart of the dark years, the record losing streak of '93–94 that long-term fans seldom mention. The ball finds Wade Chapman who roosts down to Lockett, this time getting between two smaller defenders (are there any larger ones?) and the ball before unleashing a huge 50 metre kick for goal which is still climbing as it clears the goal-line.

At six foot four and 16 stone, Lockett is the antithesis of the svelte stereotype Rules player and his imposing presence draws the crowd's attention to him, even when he is out of the action, the true leading man. Now he's sprinting into space as Derek Kickett takes a free kick in the centre. Everyone on the ground can sense Plugger's moving, but it's only Kickett who reacts, drilling the ball 50 metres into the space immediately in front of him, more magician than half-forward.

Lockett's second goal in ninety seconds takes Sydney to

an eight-point quarter-time lead. Sydney's three straight goals, as opposed to the Bombers' one goal and five behinds, sets the tone of the evening. Essendon has more chances, but the Swans convert theirs. James Hird, a boyish-looking midfielder playing in long sleeves, is dominating the open play with a flurry of marks, intercepts and handballs, but his team-mates are frustrating him with crooked kicks at goal. It highlights the importance of kicking straight in AFL—a goal is worth six behinds—and when you're not on target, that means a lot of work for very little reward.

Sydney sticks to its script with two more goals early in the second term. Lockett kicks his third from 35 metres after a neat delivery by Grant. Then the Swans show how to control the ball right through the centre of the SCG. From a Grant restart in his own goal square, Luff works the ball upfield through Kickett and Dyson. Each time there's the opportunity to rush forward, but instead the Swans steady first. Dyson picks out Cresswell on the edge of the circle. Again he sets himself, then spots Lockett unmarked, delivering him his easiest kick of the night from inside 30. At 30–12 the Swans are beginning to drive the Bombers into the SCG mud.

The Bombers bounce back, finding the one ingredient they've been missing all evening—accuracy. The Essendon forward line, with a distinct height advantage over Seymour and Dunkley, secures marks within 25 metres of goal, that not even they can miss. When Hird bombs long from 50 metres and finds a team-mate with an open goal, the Bombers are back in front.

But there is time for another plot twist before interval, with Kickett fuelling the dramatic tension. He rustles the ball around the boundary line like a sheep dog, unleashing a high kick low in the forward pocket. Cresswell flies high in the goal square and almost marks, but the ball bounces unattended, metres from goal. A muddled Swan who I can't identify follows through and just taps the ball off his instep. It isn't pretty, it isn't flashy, it isn't even tradesmanlike, but it means the margin is down to a point.

Sydney hits the lead again, O'Loughlin is awarded a free kick in front of the posts after an Essendon defender attempts a rugby pass out of the ruck. Essendon responds with a scrambling goal on the siren, but given they've had double the kicks at goal, the one-point half-time deficit is not a bad result for the Sydneysiders.

In the drizzle and rain it's hard to gauge whether the Swans are playing well. They're playing tough, they're converting their opportunities, but they are being heavily beaten for possession. What can be said is that they're playing in character: the plays that lead to the goals are the crowd-pleasing length of the field efforts, the big marks and booming conversions. It's a style of play Sydney warms to: big and brassy, a touch uncouth perhaps, but always fun to be around. It's like the kids playing the half-time match, each one groping in the mud for the glory ball, then sprinting round the boundary with their arms aloft as the siren for the main game sounds. Arrogant minnows, revelling in the hype, unconcerned what the older hands, who consider themselves the 'real McCoy', think of them.

Essendon extends its lead early in the third quarter via three behinds; then they pot two goals—both initiated by Hird. In a flash the deficit has mounted to 20 points and Sydney is beginning to feel the pressure, forcing the passes as they attempt to improvise extravagant departures from the set scenes.

When they work, it's true poetry. Kickett's magic hands come into play, scooping up a bouncing ball and finding Simon Arnott, another bit player revelling in the mud, close to the goals. Surrounded, Arnott chips to Lockett who swallows the mark in front of the posts. As Lockett walks back to prepare for his kick, the umpire signals play-on, ruling the ball has not travelled far enough from Arnott's boot. While everyone else looks up quizzically, Plugger reacts: nonchalantly hooking the ball over his shoulder and through the posts with a sweet left boot. He may look like an Easter Island statue, but his brain's 100 per cent football.

Essendon continues to miss sitters in front and by the time Sydney finally kicks its first behind midway through the third quarter, the Bombers have racked up a dozen. The conversion rates say it all: Sydney converting 89 per cent of its chances (8.1), whereas the Bombers are kicking at 40 per cent (8.12). From the stats you could surmise that the Bombers fans were having more to cheer about (20 kicks at goal to 9), but I'm here to tell you the exact opposite was the case. The only thing that gives a one-eyed fan more joy than a sweet six-pointer is a behind by the opposing team. When the behind comes from a kickable position the joy is all the greater, the miss isn't worth one point to the Bombers, it's worth five points to us! It's why Cummings, Fraser and Hird (with nine behinds between them) will be remembered as the real Swans heroes of the night.

It's when the opposition start kicking straight that the crowd goes quiet; and when Essendon takes the lead back out to 22 points at three-quarter time, you can hear a pin drop. We're tensing ourselves for the final surge back, just like Richmond a fortnight ago. But also aware that lightning seldom strikes in the same place twice.

Sydney moves Grant into attack, hoping the stand-out player for the night can have an eleventh hour impact. He immediately finds Lockett in front of the posts. Where many players bang the ball off boot, Grant caresses it, almost sliding it off the top of the instep, with total control of height, length and, importantly, swing. It means the well-versed receiver can make the allowance for the late turn, getting that vital advantage over his defender, who's effectively chasing the ball blind.

Essendon replies with the usual mixture of goals and

points and with ten minutes to go its lead has blown out to 29. Several times they have the chance to put the game away: Cresswell dispossessed by Hird while thinking about kicking for goal, Kickett losing possession across the goal face only to see the Bombers miss from point blank again. Sydney continues to gasp for air.

Then a turning point. The ball lobs up to the top of the Sydney attacking circle. Lockett and his marker, Dustin Fletcher race out to meet it. The ball bounces around the circle, out towards the boundary line as the lanky Fletcher and a marauding Plugger sprint shoulder to shoulder in pursuit. Plugger picks up momentum from a hip-and-shoulder he receives from another Bomber player, but instead of knocking the big man out of the contest, the collision merely increases his velocity.The two are haring towards the boundary line now at full speed: Fletcher in front, Lockett behind. Five metres out, Lockett gives Fletcher his own hip-and-shoulder treatment, manhandling him—not only over the line but then up and over the fence into the second row of seats a la the Junkyard Dog in *World Championship Wrestling*.

Moore Park had seen a bigger star on centre stage—when the Australian Opera staged *Aida*, they had live elephants shipped in to add to the ambience. But it is unlikely there had ever been a more damaging public performance by a large animal. Fletcher hoists himself back into the field of play, blood streaming from his face. As he's sent to the blood-bin, we get a whiff that there's some life left in the Swannies.

The crowd has barely settled when big Greg Stafford enters the fray, letting rip a booming 55 metre torpedo to register his first goal of the year. Bodies fly in the centre and McPherson snares possession, feeding Filandia who finds Grant, diving full length to rein in the mark. Grant jumps to his feet and chips to Lockett, who calmly steers his seventh goal home.

We sit tensely, aware the Swans are inching back into the game. A minute later and it's Grant with an encore performance, again giving Plugger the service he deserves, hooking a floater into him as he races around the top of the circle. When Lockett boots number eight from 45 metres we're out of our seats, sensing the Bombers' legs have turned to jelly in the scum and mud.

Eleven points behind, six minutes from time and there are no quiet passages any longer. The whole ground is on its feet, willing the Swans home, now convinced their rantings and ravings may actually count, that somehow that vital bounce will go Sydney's way.

Inevitably it's Shannon Grant, the teenager with the ball on a string, who again makes the decisive play, grabbing possession as the ball heads out of bounds, swinging a roost around his body to find Kickett just within range. Sydney loves Derek Kickett, especially when he lets rip with a torpedo—none of your deliberate measured drop-punts for goal, but the old wind up and roost, the go for glory. When they miss you know it, but when they come off the boot sweetly, there is no finer sight. The massive torp brings the Swans in to five points and they control the dying minutes.

Essendon sprays another behind from 35 metres and Sydney surges back towards the Noble stand. Luff finds Kickett in space, he steps around one defender and lets rip with another torp. We're screaming as the ball heads goalwards, but Derek has his hands on his head when the ball is signalled out of bounds.

But the Swans keep pushing into attack. A Kelly intercept sets up a midfield ball-up and Stafford taps confidently. Filandia grabs the ball and chips over the pack. It bounces short of Lockett but the big fella comes careering forward, scooping up the wet and heavy ball cleanly and handpassing to Justin Crawford. Crawford is another bit player, one who I've hardly even noticed all night. But he's no longer the fall guy as he runs into the forward pocket in front of the posts and calmly boots home the goal that we were convinced was always going to be scored. A 30-point turnaround in just ten minutes gives the Swans a one-point lead.

The ground is caught in a near-hysterical aural wave as the match enters its final minute. But James Hird, the Bombers' undisputed leading man, hasn't read the script. He snatches the ball just outside the circle and torps it 60 metres toward goal. For a horrible moment it looks like it may give the Bombers an unlikely win, but we accept the goal umpire's decision when he signals one point.

As the siren sounds one team has its heads bowed while the other is caught in a group hug. Draws are typically empty affairs, the result caught in uncertainty, a contest unresolved. Not this time. It's a draw, but it's easy to see who feels like winners. Sydney with twenty kicks at goal (14–6) split the points with Essendon who've lined up thirty times (12–18).

After most great artistic performances, it is customary to go and sip coffee and revel in the pathos, the hubris, the insight into the human condition. But not this crowd, we're pumped up on adrenalin, fuelled by those crazy final ten minutes. We wander into Friday night on a natural high, regaling all we bump into with the tale of the mad contest, demanding pubs tune in to the replay. We have our story and we spread the tale with missionary zeal: about the night when Plugger sparked a mighty comeback by throwing a Bomber into the crowd.

Introducing the Sydney Swans

1. Paul Rooooooooos: As many O's to his name as there are zeros to Rupert Murdoch's. This ex-Fitzroy captain jumped ship before his former club sunk. Wears guards on every part of his body except the neck.

3. Dale 'Shari' Lewis: Mopheaded muppet whose skill as a puppeteer shows in the forward pocket. Knows all the strings, but sometimes too lazy to pull them.

4. Tony 'Plugger' Lockett: Prototype full-forward who used to impersonate a pig but now resembles a deity. Used as a model by Easter Island sculptors.

5. Craig 'Windscreens' O'Brien: Learned how to play footy by watching a cattle dog chase a tennis ball and still leads with the face.

6. Andrew 'Spunkley' Dunkley: A strange combination of Jerry Seinfeld and a beach umbrella, Dunkley appears to be largely responsible for the influx of women at the SCG. Also very popular at the Paddington end.

7. Brad Seymour 'Centre': Theatrical performer who lives at the wrong end of Cleveland Street.

8. Daryn 'HMAS' Cresswell: Kicked crooked all the way to the semi, when he finally got his shots on target. Has not admitted many new recruits in recent years.

9. Shannon 'Hugh' Grant: Started the season looking like Uncle Fester's love child, but became a different player as his hair grew. Hasn't blown a game—yet.

11. Stuart Maxfield 'House': Moved north chasing waves, then found out he couldn't surf. Was released after a clerical error by Richmond who thought they were getting rid of Stuart Wagstaff.

12. Kevin 'Iron Mike' Dyson: Pugnacious type with a long boot and a penchant for beauty contests.

14. Paul 'Captain Courageous' Kelly: Respected political commentator and popular guitarist who can also kick a footy. Makes up for his lack of size by being ten times better than anyone else.

15. Greg 'Golden' Stafford: Developed in several local hospitals to contest the bounce for Sydney. Difficult to shake off.

16. Anthony 'Almond' Rocca: Pasty-faced mummy's boy who's gone to Collingwood so his big brother can fight his battles for him.

17. Jason 'The Reverend Sun Myung' Mooney: Charismatic youngster who tries to bring unification to the side.

18. Scott 'Soup' Direen: Thick and creamy competitor who knows how to dish it up.

19. Michael 'Mad Molly' O'Loughlin: Eager young Croweater who had had plenty of country practice.

23. Justin 'Joan' Crawford: Perennially seeks the limelight and looks younger every day.

24. Derek 'For God's Sake' Kickett: Cross between Merv Hughes and Milli Vanilli, has taken up new position as spokesperson for the Tallow Industries Association.

27. Wade 'Frankham/Mark' Chapman: Seminal assassin with a killer boot.

29. Simon Garlick 'Breath': Fruity player who eludes defence thanks to his aroma.

30. Mark 'Baysie' Bayes: Long-serving workhorse, starting to fall apart from over-use.

31. Stefan Carey: Hairdressing son of popular Australian novelist.

32. Daniel 'Elle' McPherson: From Grong Grong to the Fashion Cafe, you've come a long way baby!

34. Troy 'Lorna' Luff: Star of stage, screen and rainbow. Featured prominently in *Strictly Ballroom* especially when they sang 'Luff is in the Air'.

37. 'Bill' Clinton King: Frizzy-haired whippet who has aspirations of a life of public service. Could start with Plugger.

39. Adam 'Cobain' Hueskes: Cross-dressing rock god.

42. Simon Arnott 'Biscuits': This ginger nut with a bit of a mint slice off the left boot has been in Monte Carlo in the off-season and sleeps with a tiny teddy.

Second
Quarter

Origin of the Species

Every culture has residual prejudices, hatreds that derive from deep within the collective consciousness, rooted in instinct rather than reason. While they have differing focus and intensity, they all come down to a need to assert one's difference from the other. By pouring scorn on a different group, a tribe will draw itself closer together, identifying and revelling in the common strands that make them a tribe. It is a phenomenon fraught with dangers. In some societies these conflicts manifest in actual violence often rooted in race or religion, others in vitriolic and bigoted rantings against another group.

But for Sydneysiders there had only ever been one target of our parochialism, one group with the values and attitudes to truly disgust us. The Queenslander. We could stomach the chip-on-the-shoulder paranoia of Victorians, feeling more pity than pain from their constant attempts to denigrate us. We ignored South Australians and Western Australians; while everyone knew Tasmania was inhabited by inbreds. It was the Queenslanders, with their superior climate, thongs-and-stubbie-cooler fashion and conviction of their own worth that really got us going.

Instead of building silos, filling them with nuclear weapons and pointing them north, we developed our own way of showing this dislike. It was called State of Origin.

The Rugby League State of Origin concept was launched in 1980 after the annual interstate series had become a farce. The superior purchasing power of the Sydney rugby league competition had lured the cream of Queenslanders south, meaning they could be selected to play for New South Wales and go out and thump their compatriots each year. After a decade of one-sided walkovers, the Origin concept was launched, with the Maroons reclaiming a wealth of talent which they used throughout the 1980s to regularly belt the Blues, or the Cockroaches as we were known up North.

New South Wales had a long line of grievances against our northern neighbours. They poached our cricketers from Jeff Thomson to Allan Border in a bid to win their first Sheffield Shield. They gave the nation the Bjelke-Petersen Government, lacking the sense of irony to recognise this was really a joke which starts: 'You heard the one about the property developers who ran a government?' They turned Australia's most beautiful stretch of coastline into an amusement park of sun-stealing high-rises and Movie Worlds, making personal fortunes while depriving future generations of any stake. They marketed XXXX as beer and turned their capital city into a giant mousetrap by refusing to signpost their roundabouts.

But all of Queensland's crimes against humanity could, at the end of the day, be reduced to two words: Wally Lewis.

The balding, arrogant genius personified all we hated about Queensland. There was the cocky self-satisfaction, which would see King Wally wandering around the back play, limiting his work in defence to the odd late elbow to the head of a tackled player, only to pull out the game-breaking play in the final minutes. There was his constant haranguing of referees which spawned 'The Grasshopper' Barry Gommersal and the edifying 'Bullshit' chant of the Lang Park aficionados. Not to mention his joyful incitement of home crowds which saw more than one NSW side belted with beer cans at the end of the match. And always there were the self-centred demands for more, demands that would fuel the Brisbane conspiracy theorists against the ARL—ultimately contributing to the game's demise. Wally Lewis was the reason hundreds of thousands of Sydneysiders gathered to watch the State of Origin each year, the hopes of a Blues' win only just edged out by the desire to see one of Wally's petulant losing performances.

The Origin concept had been one of the first casualties of the Super League war. League's one-time showcase became a political football after the ARL selectors had refused to consider Super Leaguers for the 1995 series. The lack of the elite players had undermined the series, with a series of dour, defensive games, won by a Bronco-free Queensland. The games had fallen down as a spectacle because none of the players had possessed those special skills to break the arm wrestle; the Laurie Daleys and Allan Langers being sidelined for the non-event because of their alliance with Murdoch. If there was a moment of telling significance of the Death of League it was Queensland's 4–2 win in the first game of the series.

The AFL had also toyed with the Origin concept. By 1990 the series had expanded to a four-team concept involving teams from Victoria, Western Australia, South Australia and the Allies. The Allies were a conglomeration of players from NSW, Queensland, Tasmania and the ACT. But unlike League, the AFL Origin series is more a diversion than a focus for the season. There is interest in the representative games, but the crowds are smaller, TV ratings down and the games seem to lack the intensity of the club clashes. I put this down to two factors. One, in the absence of international fixtures, the players are playing for little more than pride. And two, given the prevalence of one-city teams in the AFL, that same pride is on the line every week.

For Sydney and Brisbane, in particular, the performance of the club side was much more important than the plight of a loose collection of Allies. And as I moseyed across Moore Park on a fine sunny afternoon to see the Swans take on the Brisbane Bears, I was definitely treating the game as an Origin match.

Brisbane, who like Sydney had faced serious teething problems since joining the competition in 1987, was sitting on top of the Premiership ladder. In 1995 they had made their first finals series, coming within a whisker of beating eventual Premiers Carlton in their elimination semi. Once the graveyard of aging players, the Bears were regularly filling the Gabba, with their mixture of experience and new talent, and just enough of the Wally Lewises about them to ensure that beaten teams would not remember them fondly.

Meanwhile, Sydney was clinging to eighth place. Since the stirring Essendon draw they had beaten Melbourne convincingly, before succumbing to the West Coast Eagles in Perth the previous week.

Sydney had made their first trip of the year to the MCG, totally closing out Melbourne in front of 23,000 people. The Demons, who were struggling under heavy injuries, were confined to just five goals in the entire match as the Sydney defensive line of Roos, Dunkley and Seymour again outplayed their opposites. Up the other end Plugger kicked six, Simon Garlick booted two in as many minutes in the third quarter and Luff came up with another double as Sydney coasted to an easy 44-point victory.

But it was the following week's loss to the Wiggles which had given the Sydney fans heart. In a scintillating night game in front of more than 30,000 in Perth, Sydney went blow for blow with one of the competition favourites, matching them across the field and dispelling the accepted wisdom that the Swans can't function on the larger interstate grounds. Two moments endure from the game. Derek Kickett's masterful dash around the forward pocket boundary line, mustering the ball along with his hands like a cattle dog, finally regathering and kicking truly from a sharp angle. Then Paul Kelly, bursting through the centre, taking on and beating three different West Coast defenders on a 60 metre burst, before handballing to O'Loughlin who kicked Sydney to a 15-point lead midway through the third quarter. From that point, the West Coast outplayed the Swans, finally over-running them in the last quarter to win by 36 points. But despite the scoreboard, no-one who saw the match was in any doubt that Sydney would be a genuine threat to all the top sides in 1996.

And so to Brisbane; the combination of tall poppy syndrome and tribal tendencies ensuring this will be a game played with feeling. Sydney's biggest crowd of the year, over 27,000, revel in the atmosphere which they themselves have created by turning up in such numbers.

As the players enter the arena to the loudest cheer yet, I notice the three men in blue doing something I've never seen before. They are warming up. They practise the bounce, deliberately banging the ball into the turf before surveying their handiwork as the ball arcs elegantly. They practise the throw in over the back of their head, all poise and grace.

'What are these lunatics doing?' I guffaw.

'Don't mock them so soon,' Eddie counsels. 'More than in any other sport, the umpires are tangibly involved in the game. They're not just making the technical calls, they physically get the ball moving each passage of play. Each bounce, each throw has a direct bearing on who gets possession, where they get it, how they get it. Can you think of any other sport where the umpire touches the ball?'

I think hard. 'Cricket umpires checking for ball tampering?'

'That's about as close as you will get. For a game without rules, we've got more umpires who are more involved than any other sport you can name.'

From the opening minutes, the umps show just how involved they can be; awarding O'Brien a free just outside 50 metres after he receives a high shot while attempting to mark. He lets the ball fly goalwards, but it is Lockett who makes the decisive play. Plugger simply backs into the full-back, who is poised to intercept the kick, and collapses on him, allowing the ball to pass through for six points at a height of less than a metre. It is the consummate use of the shepherd. It's Sydney by 12, when O'Brien repays the favour, lobbing the ball up for Lockett, who touches, hits up and finally marks, 30 metres out from goal.

But Brisbane replies quickly, on the back of a free kick against O'Loughlin which no-one could explain to me. It's one of the banes of the convert; being subjected to an array of unknown rules, being interpreted at pace, while sitting amongst a bunch of one-eyed supporters incapable of conceding their team could ever commit a foul. I find the toughest to be the 'Ball' calls, whether he's held it, dropped it or been caught with it. I've no idea when it's permissible to push someone to beat them for a mark, or to what lengths a defender can legitimately go to frustrate one.

'The rule of thumb is that the umpire is always right when he awards it our way and always wrong when he goes against us,' I'm told.

A concise, though less than definitive, analysis. Still, it explains the constant heckling of the umpires by the home crowd.

While I'm struggling with the technicalities, Sydney is

struggling with the competition leaders, who have kicked two more quick goals to go six points up. Sydney is competing for everything, but failing to control the ball in defence across its half-back line.

Dunkley wobbles another kick downfield. Regarded as one of the stars of the year, the Jerry Seinfeld lookalike thrills the Swans fans with his ability to snuff out big-name attackers through his tough defensive style, strong marking and ability to judge when to punch the ball free. But whenever Jerry kicks, the SCG has its heart in its mouth. The ball wobbles and skews towards its target; a completely different creature from the joyous drop-punts of a Shannon Grant or Paul Roos. This time the ball misses the pack and bounces high towards Kickett, who pulls out a typical piece of magic, punching the ball blind over his head, straight into the arms of O'Loughlin. He handballs sweetly to Luff as the Ted Mulray impersonator runs into space and sends the ball through from 30 metres. All square.

When Lockett kicks his second goal, marking an O'Loughlin kick 40 metres out, the Swans are in front. Two late kicks from Luff and O'Loughlin hit the posts and the Swans go to quarter time with a seven-point lead, which could have been more.

The game was being played with Origin-like intensity, both teams striving for the upper hand. For the first time I sense I'm starting to get a feel for the passion of the game, my interest is no longer purely intellectual. I think the turning point was the final minutes of the Essendon draw, those crazy seconds when the crowd obviously lifted the players, the fevered atmosphere seemingly keeping the ball in the air for longer and lifting players off the grass as we wiped away that 29-point deficit.

The attraction of the game is the amalgam of skills on displays, like taking the best bits of many sports. They kick like in soccer, tackle like in League, ruck like in rugby, jump like in basketball and tap the ball around like a volleyball pro. They play a positional game not dissimilar to netball, take catches that would put a slips fielder to shame and subject themselves to body contact the match of any *World Championship Wrestling* gig.

All these skills are on display as the thirty-six warriors launch themselves into the second quarter. Brisbane squares it up after Roger Merrett, a Bears institution and oldest man in the League, snaps his first goal. But three straight goals to Plugger reassert the Swans' advantage. When Sydney feeds Lockett they look unbeatable; focused and confident, knowing they will be rewarded for their midfield enterprise. While Plugger deservedly gets the accolades it's often the centre field players who make him look good.

Here's how they do it.

ONE: Luff skirts through the centre of the ground, finding Derek Kickett who nonchalantly bounces the ball and hooks it over his shoulder, straight into Daryn Cresswell's arms. Cresswell sees Lockett free in front of the posts and selflessly chips it over. The big man lunges at the ball three times but the Brisbane defender is all over him. The umpire has no choice but to award a free and Plugger threads it through from in front.

TWO: A minute later big Greg Stafford finds the blond-haired Adam Hueskes cantering through the centre. The under-rated defender has one of the most accurate kicks in the side, showing it by finding Lockett with a perfect drop-punt which leaves the Bears defender looking like a traffic cop and Plugger kicking his fourth.

THREE: Sydney attacks again and it's Kickett bringing the crowd to its feet with a full-length diving mark. He feeds Craig O'Brien on the half-forward line and the ball is sent goalwards, again dipping as it approaches the line. This time Plugger commits himself, reaches high from behind three Brisbane defenders and catches the ball at full stretch, inches from goal, giving him number five from point-blank range.

Look at the score sheets and you'd say the three goals were a fine individual effort from Lockett; but all those at the SCG knew it was the team, playing Rodney Eade's patterns to perfection, that were the real story behind the headline.

By half-time the 17-point lead has shrunk to just four points, as Brisbane again shows why it has been the competition front-runner. As the Swans take the foot off the pedal, the Bears begin pressuring them across the field with the long break approaching. One of their goals, from well outside 50 metres, keeps soaring into the Noble Stand and we know there's a lot of football left. As the hooter sounds the crowd warmly cheers two sides putting on the sort of contest that Quayle and Arko spent much of 1995 praying for.

During the break we sip beer from plastic cups, wondering how the good League players would have translated to Rules and vice versa. Laurie Daley, for example, the most talented three-quarter of his era played Aussie Rules growing up in Junee and would have inevitably made it as a star half-forward; all speed and balance. By the same token, Paul Kelly would have made the grade as a hooker or half, all guts and determination, great hands and a strong kicking game.

Every footballer, I theorise, has a mirror life in the other code, the life he would have led if he had been born in another State.

I attempt to apply my theory as the third quarter begins. One of the Swans' unsung heroes Kevin Dyson works the ball through the centre. Tanned and solid, the Swans snared Dyson from Melbourne at the end of 1995. With the longest kick in the team and a robust defensive style I speculate he would make a great centre-three quarter.

Then it's Shannon Grant, surely a rugby union five-eighth—all tactical kicking and deft working of the attacking angles—who finds Lockett unmarked in the top right of the goal circle. Lockett converts routinely.

Dunkley, whose ability under the high ball would earmark him as a full-back in league, brings the ball out of defence. Cresswell, a burly lock forward in League, runs onto the ball, using Simon Garlick, who I fancy would be a strong winger in his mirror life. Garlick snaps true from 20 metres.

Back to the bounce and Stafford, the type of guy who is fast-tracked into Wallaby sides to win lineout ball, continues to secure quality possession. A minute later the Swans are streaking downfield again with Maxfield, surely a three-quarter, running onto a ball from O'Loughlin, who reminds you of the Ella brothers and you know would mesmerise the defence wherever he was put. As the ball swings into attack again it's like a training drill and, inevitably finishes in the clutches of Tony Lockett.

And what of Plugger? There is a side of him which is your archetypal League prop forward. All brawn and bluster, able to bang lesser frames clear out of the way. He would have been the classic front-rower in the Artie Beetson mould, able to stand in the tackle and unload to the runner. He kicks his seventh and the Swans have a 22-point lead.

Plugger's repertoire of skills also highlights the limitation of our theory. How bored would Lockett be if he was forced to confine himself to League? Forced to concentrate on being a hitman/tackling bag, the big fella would have missed out on the marks and 50 metre kicks at goal. He would never have tried them because there would have been no call for him to do so; he would never have developed the skills that thrilled Sydneysiders in 1996 if he'd been condemned to a life of League.

I look across the paddock at Troy Luff and Paul Roos and can't imagine them anywhere near a League field. Not chunky enough, I think, as they sweep the ball goalwards assuredly for a Cresswell six-pointer. The Luffs and Roos are tailored for AFL, agile, streamlined, the ultimate pros.

In contrast, the prototype League player resembles a brick—all shoulders and thighs, square jaw, crew-cut. Recent rule changes making the game faster have got rid of the really big men and tall men and most players can now play anywhere between three-quarter and prop.

The bottom line is that, in all modern sport, players grow to fit their game. With increased training technologies they can actually change their bodies to fit the demands of their game, tailoring their dimensions and attributes to the coach's requirements. So you have lithe Rules players, chunky League players and cricketers with fat arses; each custom-made for their chosen sport. And so, I decide, this manifesto—like so many before it—has a limited shelf-life.

Besides, all this theorising is distracting me from one of life's little pleasures—beating a Queenslander. O'Brien kicks his second after Brisbane are penalised for holding the ball (my first ever accurate 'BALL' call), then Lockett kicks his eighth, scooping up a ball he fails to mark and banging it over his shoulder and through the posts. Garlick boots his second with a long reefing kick and then it's Plugger's turn again, kicking his ninth on the back of smart work by Stafford. It's a seven-goal quarter and Sydney is out to a 45-point lead and the spectators are all jumping out of their seats and I've forgotten Barry Gommersal and Wally Lewis ever existed, ever caused me such irritation. Queenslanders? They aren't so bad when you're 45 points up!

The final quarter and Sydney keeps the good times rolling, though the contest is long over. Lockett kicks his tenth goal—the AFL equivalent of a hat-trick of tries or a century at the crease—fielding a Kickett snap and banging it high up towards the old scoreboard. Shannon Grant drills one home from 45 metres after the Brisbane defensive line fails to clear some more Kickett magic, a crowd-pleasing combination of marks, dummies and boundary line dashes.

Lockett shocks the crowd by kicking his first behind after

ten straight goals. But it is soon a distant memory when O'Loughlin combines with Grant to find the big man 35 metres from goal. Lockett kicks truly from an acute angle and his personal tally for the day goes to 11.1–66, just two points less than the Bears. The Sydney machine continues to roll on, kicking the last three goals as a trio of unsung heroes make their mark. First O'Loughlin, high and handsome from 40 metres; then Grant, on the run from 45 and finally Dyson, after a beautiful length-of-the-field movement involving no less than seven players, all relaying downfield with aplomb.

The hooter sounds and Sydney has won by 58 points. The Sydney song rings out again and we all sing along, prompted by the words on the scoreboard. It definitely had the intensity of an Origin game, but I'm beginning to expect that every week. Melbourne at the MCG, West Coast at the WACA, Brisbane at the SCG and next week back to Melbourne.

Sydney and Brisbane have completed the AFL's missing links, forging a truly national game in its centenary year. And as we march briskly back to the Bat and Ball for the post mortems, the realisation hits me for the first time: I am not even mildly interested in whether North Sydney has beaten Balmain.

Understanding the Mullet

One of Aussie Rules' most endearing features is the prevalence of the Mullet, a bizarre hairstyle that looks ridiculous to all but the wearer.

The Mullet combines a short cut on the top and sides with long flowing locks at the back, giving the wearer a schizophrenic fashion presence, guaranteed to confuse loved ones and scare small children. In the mirror, the Mullet looks great, neat on top, with a seductive flick coming from behind the ears. From any other angle, however, it's all wrong.

It is a strange quirk of international fashion that this style is almost the exclusive preserve of elite sportspeople. In the US it's known as 'The Ice Hockey Cut', in England 'the Billy' (after Billy the Fish—the half fish/half goalkeeper character in Viz comics). It is also worn by German roadies and the stars of Asian Canto-pop. But nowhere is the Mullet worn more widely and proudly than in the AFL.

The AFL gallery of Mullets is clearly headed by Carlton's Stephen Kernahan, who just edges out Adelaide's Wayne Weidemann as King of the Mullet. But several Swans are also up there on the honour roll, led by the big three: Tony Lockett, Paul Kelly and Paul Roos. Indeed, one theory has it that if the entire Swans went the Mullet they'd all rise to these three's playing standard and be an unbeatable side.

No side has ever had the courage to undertake this risky experiment, however, although The Radiators have survived for close to twenty years on the outer suburban pub circuit proudly flaunting their Mullets.

Mullet-watching is an integral part of the football experience; identifying Mullets, devising theories about its origin and utility, designing new team strips around the dubious look. Surf the Internet and you'll find 'Mullet-watch', a locally produced home page dedicated to the look which has spawned international interest in our national game.

The big question is why? And to answer this you need go no further than *Footyzine*'s 'Footy Adviser': 'it functions well for footy, as the short anterior cut protects the scalp and prevents both hyper and hypothermia ... Body temperature is maintained at an average 37.4 degrees by the evaporation of water from the distal end of the spiked hair in the same manner that water evaporates from a canvas bag on the front of a car by the air rushing past ... The posterior long hair acts as physical conduit for air and water, creating a slipstream behind the player as he runs, which others can then take advantage of.'

The Mullet also plays an important sociological role in making our heroes more human, removing them from their pedestal and placing them back with the people. They may be gods on the field, but after the game they're just big blokes with silly haircuts.

It is perhaps notable that in the post-grand final grieving process that was Mad Monday, the first things to disappear were Plugger and Kelly's Mullets—a purging of the soul, perhaps.

The Mullet is an integral part of football. It gives football a real fashion identity, it stimulates all sort of discussions and gives the fans no end of amusement. It is a proud tradition which must not be allowed to die.

The Local Lad

When season 1996 is dissected, one of the explanations for the Swans' success will undoubtedly be the emergence of a quality tall man in the ruck. That Sydney's ruckman should emerge from the local junior competition, made him all the more integral to the team's engagement with the town. Greg Stafford had a wow of a year. Formerly a sometime starter, he held his own in the ruck against all the top sides in 1996, pulled off spectacular marks and kicked some vital goals before dominating the first quarter of the Big One.

Growing up in Sydney, how did you ever get involved with Aussie Rules instead of rugby league or rugby union like every other Sydney kid?

Funny thing you should say that; I think there's a bit of a misconception about this. It was predominantly rugby league where I grew up but there were still large pockets of Sydney that were playing Aussie Rules. It wasn't such an obscure game—there were hundreds of kids playing. I started out playing League because my brothers played League; Dad was a League man, so it was a natural progression. I wasn't enjoying it that much and a friend who lived across the road came over one night and said: why don't you give Aussie Rules a go? There was a brick pit behind our house which they turned into an Aussie Rules ground so it was all there for me.

What was the oval?

Wagner Oval. Western Suburbs, which played in SFL, relocated from Picken Oval to Wagner and turned it into an Aussie Rules ground.

What were you like as a League player?

I can't really remember, I was only six or seven. My first year in Rules was 1983 when I was nine years old. It's a bit hard at that age to know who's a star. I also played a bit of League at Christian Brothers Lewisham, as there was no Aussie Rules in the schools, but I just didn't take to the game. So I started playing Rules in 1983; I remember when I turned up there were lots of kids there, every club I played against there were kids on the bench, there was a strong network of kids and families.

So where were the suburbs where the game was strong?

In our competition, which was the St George comp, you had teams like Bangor, Miranda, Sutherland, Cronulla, Penshurst. Croydon Park and Bankstown came into it a bit later on. There was a North Shore comp and teams like Baulkham and also Pennant Hills.

Were all the kids Swans fans? Did they get you to play at half-time in the main games?

I did actually get to do that once, but I can't remember much about it. I don't know if we were all Swans fans. I remember having a bit of a fixation with Collingwood—which I think everyone does at some stage—and Hawthorn. I don't think I was a big Swans man, or boy. I think most of the kids were more likely to have fantasies of playing for Carlton, or one of the top sides like that.

How competitive were the junior games—was it more fun or war?

The rivalries, particularly between Ramsgate and Croydon Park, were just huge; it was obviously all above board, but it was just full on. In the under-9s and under-10s we were just having a kick, but when it got to 12s, 13s and beyond it was just huge. The team I played with all through juniors, from the under-10s to under-17s, we were in the grand final each year; we'd win one year and lose the next, usually it was against Ramsgate and they were super competitive.

Did they have rep football as well?

Yeah. You'd play in your Association, which for me was St George. Then you'd play in the carnival to see if you would play for Sydney. Every year, except one, I only played for St George, I never made it any further. In the under-17s I made the St George side and made the city side; we went away to play country areas elsewhere in the State for a spot in the NSW side, but I didn't make that.

Were you always a ruckman?

No, I played a bit of ruck, but there were a fair few tall kids at the time. One was taller than me and he played ruck and I normally played centre half-forward.

Do you feel a bit of a responsibility in being the Sydney-bred player in the Swans? Do you have much of an involvement with the local Juniors?

Not at this stage. If you put it in perspective I've only played one full season in Firsts, so I'm not in a position to hold any great authority with anyone. Obviously I've got the local ground basically in my backyard, so if I'm not doing anything on Sunday I wander down and watch the game. I suppose there's a certain responsibility on my shoulders to make sure the game is held in a proper light and not bring it into any disrepute. I've been back to my old school to talk to the kids, and I've done a few clinics at Wagner Oval.

Have you noticed an increase in the number of kids playing in the last twelve months?

Yeah. It really slumped between 1990 and 1995, but because the Swannies went so well in 1996 it's just booming now right across New South Wales.

What about your progression into the Swans? I saw an old Record from 1993 and you were on the list then. Was that your first year?

I was playing in the SFL, first grade, at sixteen with Western Suburbs, in the ruck. Rob Snowden approached me to come along to under-19s and have a few games there. I had four games and then the AFL scrapped the competition, so I thought that was the end of that and any chance I had to impress them was gone. But as it turned out, in 1992, which was my last year of school, they asked me to play reserve grade; so I played between Wests and reserve grade Swannies, I played about half and half. Then 1993 was my first listed year and I was fully contracted to the Swans and have been ever since.

Did you get a run in Firsts in 1993?

Yeah, when I was eighteen I had eight games, then 1994 I had about two games, 1995 I had about seven games and then I played 1996 pretty much in Firsts.

Did you feel that you had it in you to be a first grade player when you were up and down the grades?

I wasn't really conscious of the position I was in, I was just floating along really, whatever happened, happened.

They weren't real exciting times, were they?

Not really. There were three wooden spoons in a row there, including an all-time losing streak. That never affected me personally in regard to what I would do, that was just the way it was. I wouldn't let that affect me as to my ambitions to stay with the team.

Did things in your personal game just click this year or was it a case of being part of a team that was going well?

I was given greater responsibility by the coach, I was given faith and I didn't let him down. I worked pretty hard over the previous summer on fitness and that bore fruit. But it was just being given a go more than I had in the past. That's not an excuse; because I hadn't pulled my finger out at all in previous years so I probably didn't deserve to be given a go. It was just the extra responsibility, a bit more faith and everything clicked.

You also got picked for the Origin game, what was that like?

It was all right. I only played for about fifteen minutes in the game (Allies v Victoria). I was picked as first ruckman, I started the first five minutes and then I was dragged for reasons unbeknownst to me by (coach) Terry Daniher. Then I was back on for the last ten minutes. I don't know what the story was. But it's not like rugby league State of Origin where there's this vehement loyalty thing. The Victorians, sure, they're interested; but when you play for the Allies who are you playing for? Tasmania, Queensland, NSW, ACT—it's just show-pony stuff.

So you're not too disappointed that they're not going on with the Origin games next year?

Aren't they?

It's almost like the club games are Origin matches anyway. You're playing a different team every week.

I don't really believe that. I'm just playing for a club against another club, I don't even think about taking it on for NSW. If they want to bring it up and get a bit of mileage out of it publicity-wise we'll go along with it. But personally, it doesn't do it for me, it's just a game of footy. If there was another Sydney team I'd be just as keen to beat them as I am to beat Collingwood.

What was it like during that mid-season winning streak when you beat all those top sides?

That section really set us up for the year. We'd started the season badly with two losses and the way Rocket likes to do it is to get player input into the season. We broke the season up into different sections and set out our goals for each one. That run of games against the stronger sides like Brisbane, Carlton, North and Geelong, was a section. We were looking at about a 40 per cent strike rate during that period: that's two wins out of five. We would have been content with that; anything more was a bonus but we wouldn't have been happy with anything less. As it turned out we won something like five out of six of those games and we did it against the really top clubs. Our confidence just skyrocketed after that, we just proved to ourselves that we could beat anyone.

Was there any particular game when you were thinking: we're on fire here?

Yeah, a few games actually. We were on fire against Brisbane when we killed them by about ten goals. We were on fire against North Melbourne; Geelong we just outplayed them all day too.

When that stuff is happening, are you doing things differently?

A lot of different things happen during games. They ebb and flow and you often see a side who is in front, they get to a different mentality depending on the way they're playing. Sometimes they just try to protect their lead; but other times they get in front and say: you're just not going to get near me. When we were in front and bulldozing sides it was just an invincible feeling. You've got 80 per cent of the blokes all clicking together and the result is you beat North Melbourne by 12 goals.

What about your particular position in the ruck? What are the techniques?

It's actually a position going through some modifications. In days gone by the ruckman was portrayed as being this lumbering, huge bloke who just stalked around the field trying to get his hand on the pill whenever there's a bounce. These days he has to be a bit more agile and run around and be more constructive with the ball; scoop it off the ground, dishing off, kicking goals, being an extra on-baller rather than this big bloke who does nothing all day, gets five possessions and 30 hit-outs and does nothing else. Today it's 25 hit-outs and about 25 possessions that's expected of you.

In regard to the tactics; basically whenever a goal has been scored the ball comes back to the centre for the bounce. The two ruckmen run at each other and what they're trying to do is get their hand on the ball and tap it to one of three team-mates they have in the square, to be cleared. You'll find that whoever gets the most clearances out of the centre at the end of the day will probably win the game, so it's a very important part of the game. In regards to what you can do; you can raise your knee and you can raise your free hand to protect yourself, but it's a pretty grey area. Basically you can do whatever you want as long as you keep your eyes on the ball. You can't run at your opponent and completely take him out, you've got to have a feel for where he is and make use of your peripheral vision.

What about off the ball? Are you assigned a particular position on the field?

It depends on the game and the opposition. You may have a gun ruckman on the other side and you just watch him to ensure he doesn't get too many possessions and have too big an impact on the game. Other games he may be young and doesn't know what he's doing in which case I can leave him and go elsewhere. Hawthorn, for instance, has a gun fullforward, so I might just go up and block the space in front of him. It all depends on the team you're playing and the conditions you're playing.

Do you also have a specific attacking job to do? In some of those games this year you seemed pretty integral to the attacking waves.

Yeah. With the ruckman's position, which is pretty unique, you can really just go anywhere in the ground. Sometimes the game doesn't suit you to be in a particular position, but provided the opportunity's there, I can run forward and create opportunities, then go back in defence as required.

I also wanted to ask why you wear that strapping on your shoulders?

Against Fitzroy I popped the AC-joint and then against Fremantle I chipped the bone in the same shoulder. The strapping just gives a bit of extra protection.

Finally, what was the pressure like during the 1996 season?

The pressure never really got to us, it was fun all year. To Rocket's credit he's always made it pretty fun, pretty light-hearted. Mind you, when it gets down to business there's no-one more serious than him, but it was always a case of switching on at the appropriate time.

History Lessons

I wander down to the Rose Hotel on Cleveland Street on a cool Saturday afternoon to watch the Swans–North Melbourne game from Princes Park. Amidst the frescoes and bocce court a crowd gathers to watch the direct telecast. Sandy Roberts and Gerard Healy have started to become like new friends who, like all my other friends, have no taste in ties. They're tipping a North win as the 'Boundary Rider', a big bloke called Dipper who looked like Merv Hughes with an afro, does the Tony Greig impersonation, sans keys.

I pull up a stool next to Juzzo—St Kilda diehard, student of Australian poetry and itinerant drummer to the stars—as Healy gives his preview.

Juzzo looks up from his Resches: 'You know he's one of the most famous Swans?'

'Who, him?'

'Yeah. Gerard Healy. Brownlow Medallist 1986. He was a star during the Capper days, when Captain Cucumber ruled the SCG.'

Ah, history. This was a new issue for me. From what backwaters of history did this strange phenomenon called the Sydney Swans emerge? Why did this idiosyncratic, anarchic game evolve here rather than anywhere else on earth? And what of the Swans? Did they have a glorious history of countless victories or had they struggled to adapt to the twentieth century like my beloved Bears?

'Know anything about the history?' I ask.

A glazed, faraway look comes over Juzzo as he drains his schooner.

'It all began on the Victorian goldfields in the 1850s,' he intones, as the locals gather around.

'Naturally, after panning and digging all week what you'd really want to do on a Sunday was go out and clobber your fellow fossickers, let off a bit of steam. Problem was that as they had come in search of gold from all over the world, they all had different violent rituals involving a ball. You had your European soccer players, a few fallen toffs from the English public schools who played with an oval ball, some mad Italians who were still playing between villages and the Irish who had patented the ultra-violent Gaelic football.'

'So they all got together and made up their rules?'

'As was becoming necessary, with the disputes over handball and differing interpretations of the off-side rule.

'The first organised comps began in the late 1850s around Melbourne and Geelong. Thomas Wills, who actually hailed from New South Wales, was the game's founder. He wrote to the Melbourne newspapers calling for the establishment of a new game in the cricket off-season. His sales pitch was that cricket clubs would benefit by having their grounds trampled during the off-season, while the players could use the gallop too.

'The first recorded game went for three Saturday afternoons on a 990 yard field near today's MCG. Within twelve months the Geelong and Melbourne clubs had been officially established. And the rest, as they say, is history.'

'But what about the Swannies?'

'As you are no doubt aware, the Swans used to be South Melbourne. As the name implies, they covered Melbourne's inner south—the area directly across the Yarra from the Melbourne CBD across to the Port. South were personed by tough men from the docks who became known as the "Bloodstained Angels".

'Beginning in the Victorian Football Association in the 1870s, South Melbourne became a force after merging with nearby Albert Park. They won the VFA premiership in 1881, 1885 and a trifecta from '88–90.'

'Glory days.'

'Unfortunately they peaked early, although it would have been great to be around. Apparently the game was taking off, with crowds of over 30,000 at some matches.

'Then, you wouldn't believe it, the 1890s version of Super League. There'd been a long-running row between the VFA clubs over player payments and the number of teams, with a push from some of the stronger clubs for a breakaway elite League.'

'What goes around comes around.'

'The push was led by the big four of the time: Geelong, Essendon, Melbourne and Fitzroy. Collingwood offered a peace proposal for neighbouring clubs to amalgamate, which would have seen South merge with Port Melbourne, Essendon with North Melbourne and Melbourne with the Saints. Thank God, it failed.'

'Another full bench of the Federal Court decision?'

'In fact, South Melbourne was intimately involved. For the first time ever two sides finished on top of the table with equal points at the end of the 1896 season. It was decided to hold a grand final to determine the premiership: South versus Collingwood. A row blew up after the two finalists decided they'd play the decider on the day of the last round of the season. Other VFA clubs were pissed off that the draw would have to be altered and forced the date to be changed.

This alienated Collingwood from the VFA and the break-away group pounced like a News Ltd takeover team. At a meeting on the night before the grand final, the big four plus the grand finalists all voted to secede from the VFA and form their own League—the VFL. Hence, the centenary this year.'

My history lesson is interrupted by ball-up. The Swans are led out by Paul Roos, playing his three-hundredth game in the League. That's something like fifteen seasons, amazing longevity.

I vaguely remember North Melbourne as one of the glamour sides of the 1970s and am informed they've been semi-finalists for the past three seasons. They begin all over Sydney, running them around the larger field with well-drilled kicking routines and kicking two goals and five behinds. Kelly turns the tide five minutes out from quarter time, intercepting a North Melbourne clearance to shoot Sydney's first goal from 45 metres.

Quarter time and Sydney are 16 points down. I turn to my teacher. 'What of the last hundred years?'

'Hard times, my friend. Bleak winters with very few highlights.'

'Hey, you're talking to a North Sydney Bears fan, pal. We're the biggest losers of them all. Since 1908 we have won just two Premierships—1921 and 1922. Apart from a loss in the 1943 grand final we've never come within cooee of another flag.'

'Hold your skiting until I tell you the story of the Swans.' Juzzo launches into a chronology which has chilling simi-larities to the plight of the Bears.

'The Swans have always been the honest toilers of the VFL and in the early years they met with some success. They won their first flag in 1909, Charlie Ricketts captain-coaching them to a two-point win over Carlton. They also made the 1912 and 1913 grand finals, losing to Essendon and

Carlton, before the competition wound down during World War I.'

'That's right, remember the David Williamson cameo in *Gallipoli*? If only the game had taken off in Egypt!'

'South won their second flag in the first season back from the war, 1918, beating Collingwood by five points after being down 16 points at half-time. They struggled through the 1920s, but they did have the great Roy Cazaly as captain-coach. . . '

The bar breaks into a rendition of 'Up There Cazaly'.

'I know, stupid song. But the man was a legend, the first to go for the flying mark.'

'The flying what?'

'This was when they first became known as "the Swans", it was a derogatory term foistered upon South Melbourne because they had signed the cream of the interstate players. The "foreign legion" they were known as, or the "Swans". But the traditional "Bloods" or "Bloodstained Angels" was by far the preferred name.

'But no-one cared what they were being called when they won the flag again in 1933, coming from eighth position mid-season to beat Richmond by 42 points in the grand final.'

'Forty-two points? That's an annihilation. Go you Swannies!'

'And there the glory days of the Bloodstained Angels ended. They made the grand final the next three years losing to Richmond in '34 and Collingwood in 1935 and 1936.

'The only other time they ever made the grand final was in 1945 against Carlton, played at the very same ground we're watching now, in front of 63,000 fans. The game has gone down in history as "The Bloodbath". Apparently it was all fists and boots, ten players were reported with one, a Swan, being suspended for the entire 1946 season.

When they cleaned up the mess, Carlton had won by 28 points.

'Since then, not a sniff. A couple of finals appearances in the 1970s and 1980s but, get this: not a single victory in a semi-final since 1945, that's fifty-one years, the average life expectancy of a committed smoker,' Juzzo surmises, putting on a Peter Stuyvesant.

As the Sydney Swans attack the Roos' defensive line the import of my history lesson hits me. The Swans are the Bears. A couple of flags in the early days, a grand final loss around World War II and then fifty years of failure. Resurrecting my mirror life theory, I become convinced that had I been born in Melbourne rather than Sydney, I would have inevitably supported the Swans.

As we've been dredging their past, the Swans have been working themselves back into the match. Though it's hard to gauge the dynamics of a game from television, the play fractured by the need for close-up shots, it appears Roos is playing the decisive hand. Scouting the half-back, he was celebrating his three-hundredth game with a swag of possessions, intercepting countless Kanga raids and acting as the Swans' attacking link. Mid-quarter, it all clicks for Sydney: five goals in eight minutes, as the centre players consistently find the Locketts, Kicketts and Luffs within kicking range. By half-time there has been a dramatic 32-point turnaround, the Swans kicking 39 points in the term to North Melbourne's seven.

'So, Juzzo, who were the Pluggers of yesteryear?' I ask, as the teams go for the long break.

Again the drummer-philosopher avails me of his years of learning. 'The closest to Plugger would have been Bob Pratt, who played for South Melbourne in the 1930s. He was a full-forward with a true boot who kicked 109 goals in the 1933 Premiership year. He followed that up with a VFL record 138 goals the next year and 103 goals in 1935 to become the first player to kick a ton three years in a row. In all, he kicked 681 goals in 158 games, averaging 4.8 goals per match.'

'That almost out-Pluggers Plugger,' I concede.

'The other certifiable legend the Swans have produced is Bob Skilton, who was known as "The Chimp" and if you ever see a photo of him you'll understand why. As the Swans languished for twenty-five years, it was the Chimp who kept the flame burning, playing 237 games between 1957 and 1971. He skippered South for eleven consecutive seasons, winning three Brownlow Medals, captaining Victoria and finally pulling the Swans back into the semis in 1970.'

As if to honour the legends, the Swans come out firing in the third quarter. They blitz North, kicking an amazing ten goals and two behinds in the term. The goals come from all directions, as the Swans launch wave after attacking wave at the wilting Kangaroo defence. The raids are length-of-the-field efforts, all the players combining to set up some of the most spectacular goals of the year. Lockett is again prominent, setting up a personal 10-goal match tally, but he's complemented by nine other players who register goals. By mid-quarter the contest is over and we are left to marvel at the points spree.

As the pressure lifts, the topic moves to more modern history: like how did the Swans come to Sydney?

'By the 1980s South Melbourne was struggling with falling membership and crowds, poor performances on the field and little money to improve playing strength. A plan to relocate to Sydney was hatched by sections of the club concerned that the only alternative was total collapse. News of the plan leaked out during the 1981 season and a vocal group of supporters mobilised to oppose the move. They're probably the same ones in the red and white out there today.'

'Yeah, in a way they've kept their team anyway.'

'But that is to underestimate the deep resentment of Sydney from Melbourne. It would have been more palatable to the South Melbourne fans to move to Baghdad with Saddam as coach. There was a big anti-relocation push with the Keep South at South movement dividing the club. It was the full deal, protests, neighbour shunning neighbour, families fractured.

'Nevertheless, the entire Swans relocated to Sydney at the start of 1982, led by Barry Round, who had won the previous year's Brownlow Medal, and coached by former skipper Ricky Quade. Arriving with no training facilities, a reluctant playing staff and little or no interest from Sydneysiders, the Swans struggled to establish an identity, most of their players preferring to keep living in Melbourne where Aussie Rules was footy.

'Then Dr Geoffrey Edelsten arrived and the Swans established their identity all right—though it wasn't an identity that any rational individual with a modicum of pride would want to claim. After convincing the VFL to sell him the debt-ridden club for an estimated $6 million, the good doctor—who made his fortune as the king of cut-price, bulk-billed health services delivered with a grand piano in the waiting room—transformed the Swans into a sort of football equivalent to Michael Jackson's Neverland. The Swans were Warwick Capper in his tight white shorts, the doctor's young and blonde wife Leeanne in her pink sports car and the Swanettes, gyrating in G-strings whenever a goal was scored.

'The Edelsten razzamatazz produced results for a couple of years. There were some big wins and huge crowds. At one stage they scored 200 points three weeks in a row. The Swans made the semis in both 1986 and 1987, although they failed to win a game either year.

'But at the end of the day you had to wonder whether it was all worthwhile. Edelsten ended up bailing out of the

Swans and was then struck off the medical register after making some injudicious telephone calls to a hitman. Warwick ends up taking his gear off for *Penthouse*. And the Sydney Swans are left to live with the stigma of being the footballing embodiment of the evil '80s, the era when greed was good and taste was optional. It took years to recover and there were a lot of bad times in between.'

'What of those bad years?' I ask, as the game winds down, the Swans comfortably in front.

'That tale is too distressing to tell on an afternoon like this. The Swans have just beaten the competition favourites. Let's not spoil it with talk of failure,' Juzzo says as the Swans hoist Paul Roos on their shoulders celebrating their 79-point walkover and his three-hundredth game. 'This is a great day to be a Swan.'

Instead we order another round of Resches, toast the Swans and hum the theme song discreetly.

Juzzo and Eddie's
Top Ten Sydney Swans

Since 1982 the Swans have had more than their share of week-ends to forget. But every now and then a true champion has emerged, typically impressing the Mexicans more than their home city. I asked Eddie and Juzzo to pick ten of the best.

Greg Williams: This brilliant centreman was one of the greatest handball exponents of all time. Also provided great drive in attack with outstanding vision. Although always heavily tagged, 'Diesel' was consistently among the game's highest possession gatherers.

Gerard Healy: Along with Williams, Healy was a vital part of the Swans' rise in the mid to late '80s. A tireless ruck-rover with an enormous work-rate, Healy is now the AFL equivalent of Graeme 'The Trout' Hughes.

Stevie Wright: This gutsy rover won a heap of ball (and frees) by going in hard and going in often. Useful goal sneak, easily spotted by his curly red hair. No Easy-Beat.

Dennis Carroll: Experienced many highs and lows in his seven years as captain, but always remained a courageous leader and devoted captain. Coached the successful reserves team in 1996.

Mark Bayes: Classy defender and one of the longest and most elegant left-foot kicks in the game. Often used with success on the forward line. Bayes was the first Sydney Swan to play 200 games and is still going, although his 1996 season was frustrated by chronic injuries.

Barry Round: Round by name and nature, he was Sydney's first skipper who played a key role in the Swans' northern migration both on and off the field. A big bloke with a heart to match, this long-serving ruckman led the Swans to victory in the 1982 Escort Cup.

Barry Mitchell: Hardworking rover who had a knack of sneaking a vital goal when it was really needed. Went in so hard he normally looked like a mugging victim after the final siren.

Rod Carter: Mean, nasty, niggling and generally annoying. But only to opposition full-forwards. This star full-back is fondly remembered for his ability to kick the ball into play while his head was tilted sideways at thirty degrees to the vertical, earning the nickname 'Tilt'.

Paul Kelly: Beginning his career with the Swans in the dark years of the early 1990s, Kelly's whole-hearted on-the-ball performances have gained him national recognition, including the 1995 Brownlow and his selection as captain of the 1996 All-Australians.

Tony Lockett: Without question the Swans' best ever signing. Kicked more than 100 goals in his first two seasons and will kick many more for the Swans if his knees hold up. One-time bogey man whose exploits seduced thousands of new fans to the game. Kicked the Swans' most valuable point since 1945 after the siren in the elimination final.

Fan Profile

Helen Meyer

Helen Meyer was the voice for Aussie Rules in Sydney when the rest of the media was still calling it 'aerial ping-pong'. Through The Meyer Stand, *broadcast weekly on 2NBC FM, Helen charts the fortunes of the Swans, as well as providing the only coverage of the local Sydney competition. If these are not sufficient credentials, she also gets Mark Bayer to clean her office.*

I was born in Poland; raised in Sydney and lived in Melbourne for eight years after marrying a resident of the Garden State. In fact the very first date we went on was at Arden Street to watch his North Melbourne flog the team who would become my 'beloved'—St Kilda. I fell in love with the way they looked; that dramatic red, black and white appealed to my sense of aesthetics; the way Trevor Barker sailed through the air and always returned with the pill; and the fact that they were Saints.

I was first introduced to the game as a teenager watching it with neighbours on the telly. Having been raised on soccer and basketball, I found Rules to be the best of both worlds. The tempo of the game; the fluidity of the play and the consistent scoring made it highly attractive to me and my involvement was inevitable.

After eight years of the 'pure' footy life in Melbourne, coming home to Sydney in 1986 brought a few surprises. I was at the SCG from the start of season '86—but I was no fan! The glitz and razzamatazz was very unpalatable and we—mostly a hard core rock'n'roll contingent who populated the Hill—used to go, basically to barrack for the opposition. The Edelsten era really was a shock to the system for most of us and we rallied against it.

The turning point came fairly recently (round seven, 1993) when *The Meyer Window* turned into *The Meyer Stand* (named after the MCG's Ponsford Stand, which has Myer all over its advertising cladding). The show turned into a footy show because of a man called Craig Davis and we started to develop a real relationship with the Sydney club and its personnel. Mind you, I had already started to soften a bit back around 1990 when the fortunes of the Swans started to plummet. You can't help developing something of a cult mentality sharing the whole SCG with a meagre 4,000 people! With the hype and schmooze gone and something of an underdog status developing, I found myself warming to the club.

The Meyer Stand is a show that's exclusively sport, and exclusively AFL in winter and soccer in summer. We use a formula where we're connected into the local competition, the Sydney Football League, and the club St George. We look at what happened last week in football, what are the major burning issues of the week and what's happening next week. We usually have a Swans player on every week, either by phone or live, to talk about how they saw the game. My co-host is Michael Clift, who's a full-back with St George—he was also a Swans junior. We have a junior section too, which I'm very proud of, and we keep abreast of the Rams which is probably one of the most exciting things to happen to the third grade competition for many a long year.

I think a turning point for my interest in the Swans was the State of Origin in 1990 when NSW defeated the Vics at the SCG and suddenly the people of this town realised we really were a bit of a force. We had the Danihers, Rocket Carter, David Murphy, Taubert and David Bolton. Suddenly people regarded them as would-be champions.

But by 1992 we were definitely on death's door. This club was going. They were either going to merge with Brisbane or die completely. Willesee bailed them out from a financial viewpoint, but they also started a Save the Swans group and the people rallied. One of the reasons why we saved the Sydney football side was that the alternative was going to be that Carlton would play eleven away games on the Sydney Cricket Ground and that the extra money would go into the coffers of Carlton and Elliott. This was so abhorrent to the AFL community of this town that we saved the Sydney football club instead.

The losing streak was pretty damn awful, through 1992 and 1993 and 1994, we couldn't win a game to save ourselves. We had Barassi here, but we had no cohesion. We didn't have a focus point up front, we had no height, we couldn't seem to work the G at all. The constant screams were 'what's wrong with the corridor?', 'why are they afraid of the corridor?', we were always going out wide and buggering ourselves out there. And they just couldn't seem to get it right. Barassi tried to do a lot and we certainly started to develop. But Barassi is not the sort of bloke players will give their hearts to—Rodney Eade is.

I believe that bringing Lockett up here was a fundamental pivot from which everything else began. Remember, Lockett was the arch enemy of Sydney after he had smashed Peter Caven's face. I remember people ringing up and saying:

that's it, if he comes up here I'm tearing up my membership. Lockett came up and from the word go people fell in love with him; people found him to be something so attractive; and despite being so controversial, he decided to come. Now remember Lockett's mindset. All those years with St Kilda, one of the most derided clubs in the comp, he was constantly being bagged, constantly being abused. He learned to use that negativity to put wind in his kicking sails and boot it like a champion for the Saints. Now he took that formula to Sydney. In the beginning there were people who hated him and derided him, but as soon as he started kicking goals for us, that hate turned to love because all Sydney is interested in is a winner and Lockett started to win games for us. He was finishing off what the rest were doing, but no-one else was able to do what he did. We didn't have a full-forward before him.

I think that we Sydney supporters suffer from the bad PR of being a bunch of bandwagon followers. There seems to be a general perception around the country that Sydney people don't know anything about Australian Rules. They're not going out there for the game, the sheilas are out there for the shorts and the blokes are out there for the piss-up. They're actually mistaking us for the fans of ten years ago. In the mid to late '80s, when we were averaging crowds of 25,000 to 30,000, very few of those people were out there for the game, they were there for the image.

Today, all you have to do is sit in the stands and you hear what people are saying—they are most definitely there for the game now, they have really embraced this team. Admittedly we're winners at the moment and it's a very grey area as to what's going to happen next year, but they are definitely developing a relationship with their club. They're starting to really understand the players and the play and they're getting their heads around the rules, and they're encouraging their kids to start playing. We can see from junior development where we're going, that wider Sydney wants to participate in this sport and that's the crucial difference between now and ten years ago. Then we had to beg, steal and borrow to get a development officer into a local school. Now they're petitioning the Education Department to actually bring clinics into schools.

The Lean Years

This question of the Swans' dark days is toying with me. I know from the snippets of Aussie Rules that permeated the Sydney media over the years that the Swans had experienced some very lean years. Years when there were more changes of season than Swans victories. Years when a 40-point loss was a close thing. Years when things got so bad and crowds so low that the AFL seriously thought about packing up and forgetting about Sydney altogether.

The knowledge of these lean years is the only thing that has detracted from my joy of cheering the Sydney wins in 1996. As a long-time Bears fan, a perennial loser, I had always frowned on those who merely backed a winner. We called them 'bandwagon cowboys'.

The bandwagon cowboys were a breed who were easy to pick, using a very simple, foolproof test. All you needed to know was the person's age and favourite football team. For instance, anyone born in the 1950s or very early sixties who backed St George was a bandwagon cowboy. Between 1965 and 1968 it would be anyone who supported Easts. People born between 1968 and 1972 it was Manly or Parramatta. The link was between the age that a person first got interested in the game (normally between seven and ten) and the Premiers of that season. If the two correlated you knew you had someone who would jump, someone whose preferences were deeply rooted in the results rather than the love of the game. It was cold comfort to a Bears fan, but gave us a sense of moral superiority that only just failed to outweigh the depression of another losing year.

With this historical baggage though, it was hard to follow the Swans' successes without feeling you had cheated just a little bit, that you hadn't made the sacrifices to really enjoy the success. I needed to know more about the details of these dark, neglected years; maybe in the hope that it would give me a true grounding in the Swans experience. I wanted a fast-track, crash course in losing.

And so there was only one topic of conversation when I again ran into Juzzo, perched on the same bar stool in the Rose Hotel, later in the week.

'Look, mate,' I sidle up to him. 'I know you're on cloud nine with this winning streak and everything; but I'm being held back by my ignorance. Every week when we sing the victory song, I feel like an imposter, some blow-in with no moral fibre. I need to know and I need to know now: what happened during all those years when no-one turned up to the SCG in winter?'

My persistence had paid off, for Juzzo was in a reflective mood.

'OK, I'll tell you. But there are two rules you must promise to observe. You buy the Resches and we don't mention Warwick Capper—I still have nightmares about the fruit he used to wear down the front of his shorts.'

No worries; I order a round and purge Captain Cucumber from my memory. Juzzo leans into his delivery like a weekend golfer hacking away at his handicap.

'You can slot the lean years neatly into the period from 1987, the last time the bloke we're not going to mention and his cohorts postured their way to the finals, right through to round three, 1996. In those nine years there were few highlights, even fewer wins, just a lot of pain and frustration.

'At the lowest point in mid-1993 you would have been lucky to have 4,000 turning up on match day—and those of us who did went there for a bit of solitude, rather than with any thoughts of seeing a football team. We were there by default really, all supporters of other clubs whose need to watch a game of footy was greater than the chagrin of turning up to watch the most ridiculously showbiz team in the code.

'So half the supporters are there in different colours and, when it was a glamour Melbourne side like Carlton or Geelong, there would be way more of the other team's supporters there than Sydney fans. At the end of the game you'd run the gauntlet of hostile fans from the visiting side sitting around the Hill just to get out of the ground and away from that day's debacle. You were a foreigner in your own home ground. In a few words it was a very depressing, humbling experience.'

'So was there any joy in it at all?' I wonder.

'Oh, there was the peace and stillness, I suppose. All the way up Cleveland Street right into the ground not a soul in your path; free chairs in the Bat and Ball, no queues, no supporters, no need for snack bars and not a thought of turning a buck out of merchandising. There was also a sort of camaraderie between us all; we'd sit and drink and grimace as the Swans fumbled their way around the paddock, but you didn't exactly get too caught up in the excitement or anything.'

'I know what you mean. All those years traipsing to Bear Park, you were just cruising for a bruising. You knew deep down, beneath all the false hope and expectancy, that this was the way your life was. You were one of those guys who supported a losing team.'

'It takes the pressure off actually. Imagine how gut-wrenching some of those years would have been if you actually thought you were a guy who supported a winning team. We were people who knew our place in life and were resigned to our fate,' Juzzo agrees.

'The one group who always stood out were the old folk, mainly women, who occupied the area in the MA Noble Stand directly behind the goalposts. This group was dedicated to the craft of barracking with a fury that belied their age. Their speciality was giving a verbal bagging to the opposing full-forward in terms which would shock even the knuckle-dragging Richmond supporters. During quiet passages of play, or when the ball was spending a lot of time up the other end, they would knit; usually scarves or jumpers in red and white. They could start and finish a full-length scarf in one sitting on a really bad day. But no matter how boring the game, these shrill voices of experience could be heard all the way across the paddock.'

'What I can't understand, though, is what changed after 1988? Why did things suddenly turn so bad?'

'Well Dr Geoffrey's demise is well chronicled. The good doctor got caught organising a hitman to knock off a business associate over the telephone. Lousy PR. Lost the medical centre, lost the footy team, lost Leeanne—proving that there's always some good that comes from any personal tragedy.

'You've also got to remember that Edelsten went belly up at about the same time as the stock market crash. This not only knocked out the Swans' owner, but the bulk of the yuppie Swans fans who had been loading the boots of their BMWs with chicken and champagne for the past two years. Again, good riddance.

'But there was a down-side too. Sydney was more exposed to the crash than any other club in the League because they had dabbled in private ownership. The late '80s really underlines the folly of this type of structure—and may serve as a warning to Super League.

'Private ownership ties a club's fortunes much more closely to the plight of its financial backers. When they're on the skids, so is the club; and when the whole economy is on the skids, they don't have a hope. It almost guarantees that any privately owned club will have high points and low points during the eight-year economic cycle; when the indicators are up, the stands are full and the best meat that money can buy is running around the paddock. But it's like the Sea Bubble, after whom some believe South was named; when it bursts and the gold dust finally clears, there's absolutely nothing there.

'Now your public club won't be injected with huge cash flows during the boom years, the type of money which allows Sydney to purchase half the Geelong side, as it did one season. But it does give you a firmer base to work from: a strong base of members who have a personal stake in the club, whose support isn't reliant on the ASX listings or this month's pork belly projections. In really simple terms, it's about having a soul.

'Of course, the Edelsten withdrawal was only the beginning of the decline. The Swans reverted to AFL ownerhip, then they were bought out by a glitzy consortium which included a bald man who had once made a drunken disgrace of himself on national television— perfect for a club owner's curriculum vitae.

'They battled on season after season, emptying the wallets of their owners relentlessly. To their credit the owners stuck with them as they picked up the wooden spoon three years running—1992, '93, '94. Along the way they snared the Swans' longest ever losing streak, twenty-seven games on the trot through 1992 and 1993.

'As things continued to deteriorate, rumours that the Swans would be wound up began to circulate. We're talking early '90s here. There were crazy notions that the Swans would be relocated to Canberra, or to Tasmania—I think Fremantle was even mentioned. What was the point? They were a dud team, giving financial backers zero return. There were no crowds turning up. And the once strong Sydney AFL competition was also on the skids, with no interest in juniors and schools.

'You see, Aussie Rules had actually been played in Sydney since the 1890s and had developed strongholds, particularly in St George, Western Suburbs and the Hills District. The local league had its own TV show, the Sydney grand final was telecast live and you'd get 10,000 people to the end-of-year play-offs. Problem was, when the Swans moved to Sydney there was no integration of the VFL team with the local clubs; and the Swans' presence actually undermined the local comp, taking the limited sponsor dollars and really entrenching the competition as a second tier operation.

'By 1992 it was fair to say that Aussie Rules would have been stronger in Sydney if the Swans had never come here in the first place. People were looking for a way out and there was the very real prospect that they would fold.'

'What I don't understand,' I interject, ordering another round, 'is why people kept turning up?'

'It's that losers psychology we were talking about earlier. The one joy in backing a dud team is that those rare victories, which fans of other teams would shrug off as run of the mill, keep a certain lustre. It's like the diamond you find on the cellar floor—it glows so much brighter than in the jeweller's shop. There are games that were absolutely breathtaking and there were players who battled through those dark years with as much guts and glory as any flag-winner.'

'So when did things hit rock bottom?'

'Without doubt it had to be during the losing streak. It was truly a diabolical run, which included some of the worst shellackings football has seen. I remember one game in early 1993, when North Melbourne kicked 36 goals against us, but it was just one of many long afternoons. That was just after they'd sacked Gary Buckenara as coach mid-season. The results had got so bad the poor bastard was being booed by the spectators whenever he came onto the ground at the breaks. When Essendon gave the Swans their fourth straight thrashing at the start of '93—their twentieth consecutive loss—Buckenara was finally shown the door.

'By this stage the club was again in trouble off the field too: falling support putting real pressure on its finances. The AFL offered support on the basis that control reverted back to them, they would run the club with the previous owners as directors. Once under AFL control, the Two Ronnies got together and decided to build a football team.'

'The Two Ronnies?'

'Ron Joseph, the former North Melbourne boss, was appointed the Swans' chief executive when the AFL came on board. He came up to Sydney with AFL Commissioner Allan Schwab, who was found dead in a Kings Cross hotel weeks into the new job, sparking further talk of a curse of the Swans. Undeterred, Joseph turned his energies to actually building a real football club, rather than settling for an out-of-town venue for Melbourne players. He built a gymnasium for the players, a social club, an entire system to make the Swans feel at home in Sydney rather than merely Melbourne refugees. Most importantly he recruited Ron Barassi, the legendary motor-mouthed king of motivation, who'd coached countless Premiers with his colourful, vitriolic techniques. The two teamed up and set about building a team from the bottom up.

'One of things that helped Sydney was that, as they were always losing, they were given priority picks on the end-of-season draft. Now, while they had always been in the position to secure a few big names, Barassi helped them chose more wisely in the second and third round choices, the unknown teenagers who could one day be stars. In those years they picked up kids like Wade Chapman, Shannon Grant and Michael O'Loughlin, no-names, who only the shrewdest of judges would have earmarked as future champions.

'Then, of course, there was the one champion they signed, the player who more than any other has turned things around.'

'The big fella?'

'Correct. Mullet-man, the Plugmeister, call him what you will. When it was announced that Sydney had signed Plugger, many Swans supporters were disgusted. There was this history of bad blood between Lockett and Sydney, peaking in 1993 when he punched out Peter Caven at the SCG, smashing his nose like an eggshell. Then there was that celebrated incident the same year when a wag let a live pig onto the field with Lockett's number painted on its back!

'But it wasn't just that incident which upset us. It was the whole philosophy behind the purchase—Sydney was trying to buy its way out of trouble again, signing up the aging megastar, rather than building a team of its own.

'Remember, Lockett was the wrong side of twenty-nine, had a dicky knee and couldn't be trusted to control his temper. On paper he looked like your typical show-pony, who would surely take from the club more than he would give. History was punctuated with cautionary tales of expensive players that the club couldn't afford, who were showered with money as the local kids were yet again neglected, eventually to leave for greener southern pastures.

'Lockett's signing made no objective sense but, from the moment he waddled onto the SCG and booted his first six-pointer in early 1995, Sydney had turned the corner. It wasn't just the hundred goals a year that he kicked. Sydney loved Plugger. The crowds gravitated to him, as did the younger players. Twelve months later, Craig O'Brien was following him north from St Kilda, underlying the fact that Sydney had become an attractive destination rather than just the venue for a well-paid tour of duty.

'At the end of 1995 Barrassi decided to step aside as coach, but he's still playing an active role in the club. He also played a part in the decision to appoint Rodney Eade as coach this year—and that's turning out to be a buy every bit as good as Plugger.'

'So was it just good recruitment and a few wins that turned things around?'

'Partly, but not solely. You've also got to say that the game is now in a far better position to capitalise on this year's popularity than it was in the '80s. In 1994 the AFL embarked on a five-year business plan to develop the national game. Obviously Sydney was integral to this and was allocated more than $1 million to develop junior football, the project being administered by the NSW AFL. Now this wasn't just a bunch of old hacks sitting around waiting for lunchtime; it's run by certified legends Craig Davis and Rod Carter, who push the game through the schools, the junior grades, all the way up to local and country competitions. In 1986 the Swans' success was like winning at the casino. This time round it's more like we're reaping the interest from savings we've already put in the bank.

'The one other initiative you may have noticed this year is the NSW–ACT Rams.'

'Yeah, I've seen them play a few curtain raisers.'

'This is probably the most important of all the growth strategies. For the first time NSW is fielding an under-19 team in the national competition, made up from the best kids in Sydney, Canberra, Griffith and Wagga. If you look at the ladder, they are right up there near the top at the moment, performing beyond everyone's wildest expectations. And the important thing is this: these are the kids who will keep the Swans strong, way after Plugger has kicked his last goal.

'And so it is the Rams who are the real happy ending to this long and depressing tale. Join me in wishing them health and prosperity!'

We drain our last schooner on a decidedly up note, part company and head off into the night.

There have been many parallels with my Bears in this story, enough low points for me to feel like a fellow traveller; the hardships I have endured sufficient to qualify me for honorary Swan-dom. The story of the turnaround also has its parallels. Norths' renaissance came in the early 1990s under the chairmanship of David Hill, who scored the trifecta in management challenges, heading up the State Rail Authority, then the ABC, then the Bears. (To prove his stomach for a lost cause, Hill's next job would be as the boss of Australian Soccer.) His reign was characterised by bold and imaginative administration, a preparedness to extend the notion of what was a football club. In many ways, Hill was to the Bears what the Two Ronnies were to the Swans.

The real divergence between the Swans and the Bears came when you looked to the future. The Swans have given themselves a base to grow and thrive, through the schools and juniors right up to the elite levels. The Bears, in contrast, are locked in by history and geography, a suburban team in a game with pretensions of national and international status. No matter which way they had jumped in Super League, their long-term chances of survival without an amalgamation or merger were the slimmest of slim.

Thinking about the two teams as I wander home up King Street, I become more convinced than ever that I'd made a good decision. I had managed to switch codes, but do so in a way that kept a sort of emotional consistency about the whole process of supporting a team. I was still backing a side with a long history of failure, incompetence and disappointment. But I had added one vital factor to my fan's armoury in the transaction, a factor essential to any long-term commitment. Hope. Hope that at some time, somehow, this team of losers would turn the corner. Hope that these ugly ducklings would one day truly become Swans.

Juzzo and Eddie's Top Ten Games (1982–95)

There have been some tough times for the Sydney Swans; but there were also those occasional wins which are all the more satisfying for their rarity. Here are ten of the best.

Round One, 1982 V Melbourne

After the brawling that preceded the move up north, captain Barry Round led the Bloods/Swans to their first match in this strange football-free city. It was a cracker. Sydney led Melbourne by at least two goals at each turn. In the end the Mexicans are banished from the SCG by almost 40 points. For the rest of the season, Sydney was in the running for a finals spot up until the last home and away game; it was a performance rarely matched in the next fourteen years.

Round 15, 1983 V Fitzroy

During round three of 1983, Fitzroy—on to one of those rolls that made them a force to contend with in the early '80s—had beaten Sydney by 9.5. By Round 15, they faced a more in-form Sydney. Leading by 31 points at the big turn, the Roy-Boys were stopped in their tracks, scoring four behinds while Sydney pulled away; first by two, then by six goals in the last two quarters, the Swans finishing with a 30-point win. By the end of the season it was clear the loss was an aberration, with Fitzroy finishing third, while the Swans were getting used to their comfy niche in the eleventh spot.

Round 16, 1986 V Essendon

For the first six weeks of season 1986 the Swans looked exactly the stuff, winning every game by more than 10 points. This was the best start to a season since 1936. The club was flush with funds, new talent had been bought and they began to attract large home ground attendances. In round 16 they were up against the Bombers at the SCG. For each bell the Swans managed to put on at least five goals, coming up 61 point winners. They finished second on the ladder at the end of the home and aways, being the first team outside Victoria to make the finals.

Round 17, 1987 V Essendon

1987 was another dream/horror year for the Bloods as money continued to be thrown around. Sydney came up with some extraordinary results—in three consecutive matches they scored more than 30 goals, beating West Coast by 130, Richmond by 91 and Essendon by a staggering 163 points. The last of these saw the second biggest score in history, with the Swans putting on eight goals to the Dons' two in the third quarter and thirteen majors to one in the last. Captain Cucumber was at the top of his form, finishing the season only second to some Saint called Lockett for top goal-kicker.

Round 16, 1988 V Hawthorn

Despite some thrills against Melbourne, Fitzroy and St Kilda in the 1988 season, Sydney really fired one off against Hawthorn. Midway through their run as goal monster of the '80s, the Hawks had not lost a game in seventeen rounds between 1987 and 1988. Sydney and Hawthorn met in round 16 and it wasn't a game that promised much for the Swans. The Sydney forwards waited until the second half before they pumped up the volume, putting on 8–5 to the Hawks 1–5 in the third quarter and coming out 51 points ahead after a quarter played almost entirely in the Hawks' goal square. This year also featured the ignominious game against Collingwood when the Sydney score stayed at one very lonely goal until the third quarter, when it was doubled.

Round 1, 1990 V Carlton

By 1990 the 1986–87 shine had come off the Swans and they were mired in financial difficulties, ending the previous year second from the bottom. But the first game of 1990 seemed an incredible return to form. South/Sydney had not beaten Carlton at Princes Park for twenty-five years and, by half-time, it looked like staying that way for another quarter century. At the big turn the Blues led by six goals; in the third, though, the Swans put on six to Carlton's two. The last quarter was a repeat of the third, with Sydney winning 15–14 to 14–15, the sweet miracle victory due to Barry Mitchell's goal from a mark just out of the goal square with fifteen seconds to go.

Round 13, 1993 V Melbourne

Two years later and the Swans are in the twilight world now known as 'the Great Depression' under the misdirection of Gary Buckenara. Sydney had not won a game in twenty-seven rounds, but the jaded and diminishing fan base was treated to a rare mid-season spectacle against Melbourne. In front by three points at half-time, Sydney kept the Redlegs to a single point in the third quarter while adding 64 of its own. Although the Establishment managed six majors in the last, Sydney's two-year drought was broken by 40 points.

Round 22, 1993 V Carlton

So rarely had Sydney won games in this period that what supporters were left grabbed at any old result as confirmation that a comeback was possible—before the team was moved to Wagga. Round 22, 1993 at Princes Park yielded such a result when Sydney clawed its way back from a 4–2 deficit at half-time, for a one point loss at the siren. A year later they won a game.

Round 21, 1994 V Carlton

Barassi had bought some stability back to the Swans by 1994 and Sydney gave him four wins for the year—a 400 per cent improvement on 1993. In contrast, Carlton had not lost a home and away game since the 1992 season began. Sydney matched everything Carlton threw at them at the SCG, remaining neck and neck until the last quarter when the Swans finally edged ahead by a goal and a pair of points.

Round 5, 1995 V Adelaide

Sydney was at last crawling out of the cellar in 1995. Round five against Adelaide gave them the second of the eight victories they would record that year. Adelaide got away to a giant start, putting on 5–7 in the first term. By the fourth quarter most of the spectators were headed for the car park, assured Adelaide's 3–1 lead would grow in time-honoured fashion. What they missed was a portent to the following season's otherworldiness—Sydney scored so early and often throughout the fourth that the goal umps barely had enough time to put the flags away between shots. In reply, the Crows put on a solitary point. End result, Sydney's 11–9 final quarter spree left Adelaide 57 points down.

Swans Seduce Sydney

Early July and everyone's a Swans fan.

Sydney has established itself in the top four with some rousing performances. Since the North Melbourne runaway they have thumped Footscray by 46 points and Carlton by 11. The only sour note of the big Footscray win, played in front of 22,000 at the SCG, was Wade Chapman breaking his foot, after again being one of the best players on the ground. But there was no downside when the Swans knocked first-placed Carlton off its perch the following week. Despite being 11 points down at the final break, the Swans booted six final quarter goals to embarrass a string of complacent commentators who had given up on them. The win was Sydney's third against a first-placed team (following North Melbourne and Brisbane) and confirmed its status as genuine semi-final contenders.

Now the Swans are on everyone's lips

Saturation media coverage sees Plugger posters in the tabloids and live crosses to Swans training for the TV sports reports. Dinner parties are hijacked by debates over whether Tony Lockett is sexually attractive (verdict: maybe if he tried a new hairstyle). Interest in junior football surges as the youth of Sydney discover new heroes. The wave of interest transcends age and class lines. Yuppies scramble for seats in corporate boxes while the working people arrive early to get the best spot in the Concourse.

Some hatch conspiracies that News Ltd is pushing the Swans as part of a destabilisation strategy, an underhanded attempt to highlight the ARL's weaknesses. But it is the quality of the two competitions which is dictating the column centimetres. Every time newcomers tune into a Sydney Swans game, they go away having seen a rousing display by a committed, skilful outfit boasting one certified legend and an array of demigods. If they actually turn up to a game they witness a spectacle transcending the image from the television: a fast, sweeping story with magic moments aplenty.

Meanwhile Rugby League is struggling. Crowds stay away as their sides go through the motions, the majority of games passionless thrashings, victims of the widening talent gap. Even with the game in crisis, rich clubs like Easts continue to raid the weaker clubs' talents. When word leaks that South Sydney's only star player will join Manly next year, it's not just a case of deja vu (Manly-Warringah was built on the poach), but League eating itself. I stay away from the under-strength State of Origin series, but am told the games reach no great heights; dour forward defensive affairs, with most tries coming off kicks.

A dive in viewer numbers forces Nine to scrap its Sunday night replay, instead relaunching Monday Night Football, a failed concept first tried in the early 1990s. The match of the round will be transferred to Mondays, to be played under lights in front of a packed house. In the lead-up to the first game, the ARL launches a desperate promotion to get the punters to the game. Everyone I know has been given free tickets and they all want to give them away. You can get tickets everywhere. Buy a Big Mac, get a ticket. Call up breakfast radio, get a ticket. Walk through Martin Place at midday, get a ticket. No need to ask and yet you still shall receive.

In stark contrast, tickets to the Swans game are in hot demand. Geelong is one of the AFL glamour clubs, grand finalists in 1992 and regular finalists since then. They boast a legion of AFL stars like Gary Ablett (aka God), Billy Brownless and Garry Hocking. By Friday the game is a sell-out and what used to be considered the world's most useless profession: a scalper at a Swans game, has become a viable career option. During the week Swans members have received letters urging them to arrive to the game early, as seats may be scarce. And so we arrive ninety minutes before the bounce, bypassing the Bat and Ball to get some of the last remaining seats in front of the Noble Stand.

The logjam has been caused because SCG members have jumped on the bandwagon too. These are the people who are put on the waiting list at birth by sports mad parents. In previous years they had stayed away from Aussie Rules, the Swans striking a deal to give their members access to the SCG members' areas. Now they were all coming along for a piece of the action. As ball-up approaches there are no seats left. In the ultimate rebuff, members are advised that the ground is full, but they are welcome to take a seat at the SFS, the home of League, to watch the game on the big screen. We snigger complacently.

The SCG is a buzz of colour and noise. Ignoring the pre-game sheep-dog trials, I focus on the atmosphere. It is the first full house for a Swans game in a decade. A sea of people rings the field, none of the familiar gaps of plastic seats, as the players run out. A roar goes around the ground as Lockett bursts through a 'Thank You Sydney' banner. Then we jeer Geelong, led out by God, perhaps the ugliest player in the AFL, all straggly hair, bald spot, ill-fitting moustache and crooked nose.

The atmosphere of a full house is altogether different. There's a sense of event, an exclusivity that isn't there when there are empty seats. You wonder where the sea of red and white comes from—how have 30,000 materialised in the past three months making the 10,000 people who turned up to that first Dockers game seem like an different season entirely? These are the people who have tuned into a Swans game on telly and decided they want to see more—maybe it was the North Melbourne or Carlton games, or the match from Perth when the Swans lost bravely, the madcap Essendon draw or the annihilation of Brisbane. Regardless, they're all here today and with their presence comes an atmosphere never before experienced in Sydney.

It's fourth versus fourth with the winner to move to second spot on the ladder. But the match is also being billed as the first test of Sydney's finals credentials. Matching up against a quality team in front of a full house will give the Swans their first flavour of the pressure cooker atmosphere of finals football. It is accepted wisdom, from all of us who read the sports pages, that Sydney has to perform today to show it is a genuine contender rather than a pretender.

All pumped up, the rovers scuffle before the game has even started, and the umpire bounces play away while they trade niggles. Rocca gets an early shot at goal, but kicks his customary behind. Then Geelong's Peter Riccardi, looking like a throwback to a '70s glam rock band, strides through the centre to give the Cats their first goal.

Sydney keeps building attacks with Roos and Direen setting up play at the back, but it breaks down through poor delivery or crooked kicking, Kelly and Cresswell register two more behinds. Still, it's engrossing footy, every man in a tight contest with his opponent, the play sweeping from one end of the field to the other. The Cats are putting some fluid passages together too and when Billy Brownless kicks a massive goal from outside 60 metres and it's Geelong 12–3, ten minutes from quarter time.

Down in front of the Noble Stand, Tony Lockett is doing all that he can to work himself into the match, constantly moving ahead of his marker, preparing for leads while the ball is still 50 metres away. He lunges at a Derek Kickett speculator right in front of the posts, but the ball drops short. Then Jason Mooney, on for the wayward Rocca, swings the ball into the square; this time it sticks and 44,000 Sydneysiders roar as Plugger bangs it through the posts and into the top deck of the Noble.

Sydney hits the lead when Maxfield runs onto a loose ball, lost by Kickett as he shaped to snap for goal. The blond flier grabs the pigskin, turns and hoiks a high ball through the posts. From the restart centreman Kevin Dyson gains possession and relays to Mooney at the top of the 50 metres. Lockett has begun to sprint away from the full-back before the ball has even reached Mooney and by the time he dives full-length to mark, he's travelled 30 metres at full pace. After the normal socks and sluggo adjustments, he threads the ball through clinically. When Craig O'Brien, the perfect foil to Lockett, kicks his first goal right on the quarter time siren after a Geelong defensive error, Sydney is up by 16 points. A four goal turnaround.

The second quarter begins with the same intensity. Within seconds, Kelly has a sniff, soccering the ball off the ground for a point. Geelong comes back manfully, attacking desperately on the edge of the Sydney 50. A Cat senses a hole and takes off towards goal, but he's pulled down by Maxfield in a flying tackle round the waist. Direen swoops on the ball and sends it out to Troy Luff, unmarked in the centre square. The roar builds as the SCG's favourite battler runs 20 metres before sending the ball on a 40 metre trip to goal.

The Swans are dominating across the field, clearing the

ball from their own defensive line with a minimum of fuss. Three sharp deliberate plays and they're back on the attack. This time it's Hueskes, working the ball from his defensive zone, an assured handball to Dyson and on to Shannon Grant who picks out O'Brien 60 metres downfield. Most players will take stock when they get a mark within kicking range, steadying themselves before making their assault on the goalposts. Not O'Brien. He nonchalantly turns and lets rip with a 50 metre torpedo that sends the Swans to a 29-point lead.

Geelong finally kick one, but Dale Lewis replies with a soft goal after being left unmarked in the fifty. Kickett gets a standard free, stands around looking for a lead and sees Lewis alone, simply forgotten by the markers. Sydney maintains the upper hand, peppering the Cats with three consecutive behinds. Under pressure, Geelong struggles to get the ball out of defence, passing back and forth across the line rather than making a decisive play. Hocking handballs blind straight to Lewis, who ambles towards the posts to kick his second goal.

It's five minutes to half-time when God finally gets a touch. But it's only a touch. The Messiah of Geelong has been missing in action all afternoon, neutralised by the dual attentions of Andrew Dunkley and Brad Seymour. Now the ugly man breaks through a scrap in front of the Geelong posts, just getting a boot to the ball as it rolls towards the line. Sydney again replies, this time through Mooney.

A suspect penalty for tripping gives the Cats another goal on a platter but it's Sydney by a whopping 36 points at half-time when Maxfield goals right on the siren. In a sequence highlighting the toughness of the Sydney forward line, Lockett surges to mark, missing the ball by a whisker. The big fella hauls himself up off the turf, grabs the loose ball and storms cross-field, shrugging off two defenders and sending Maxfield into the clear. It's all guts and glory as the ground record crowd rises to cheer its team as they go to the long break.

'But isn't this just a passing phase?' Gesturing at the packed stands, I throw out the fishing line at the half-time break.

'Absolutely,' Juzzo offers. 'I was here in 1986 when the ground was full. Everyone loved the Swans. Those times are remembered for Warwick Capper, Dr Geoffrey, the Swanettes; but the razzamatazz was not what got the crowds in. It was far simpler—they were winning games. Those huge crowds in 1986 were in the middle of an amazing winning streak; they went three weeks in a row chalking up 200 points. Everyone loved the Swans when they were doing that.'

'Fair weather friends.'

'Precisely. I'm prepared to wager that if the Swans lose five games in a row we'll be back to 10,000 people,' Juzzo surmises.

'I disagree,' Eddie interjects. 'There's a fundamental difference between 1986 and 1996 and that's the different management of the club. In 1986 it was a private concern. Let's face it, it was Dr Geoffrey's plaything.'

'I thought that was Leeanne's job.'

'Whatever. The club was a product of the '80s and reflected the times. It was his, not ours. Today it's a totally different situation; it's a public club with 10,000 members, a base that's sure to grow if they keep playing like this. That's a huge number of people identifying with the club as "their club"—and don't forget the 1,500 or so members in Victoria. This is the foundation for a long-term powerhouse, not a flash in the pan.'

'I still think there's a risk,' says Juzzo. 'Sydney is a city of fashion over habit; fun over commitment. People turn up to events because everyone else does: why else would RAT parties have succeeded? How could you get 40,000 in the

Domain to hear the fat lady sing? Sydneysiders go where other Sydneysiders go. The draw is the atmosphere which asserts that they are part of Sydney, the world's most beautiful city.'

'So the challenge is to keep the magic going,' I offer.

'Precisely. The Swans have the potential to become one of those identifiers, something that defines us as Sydneysiders. If they can stay around the top eight for the next few years, I see no reason why they won't have fans for life.'

'There's a missing factor here,' I chip in. 'Sydney is like a lover on the rebound. We've walked out of our long-term relationship with rugby league and we're looking for someone new.

'Now there are two things about lovers on the rebound. One, they demand the utmost respect, no mucking them around like the last guy did. That's why the stuff-up with the full house and the members not getting seats is a bit of a concern.

'Second, if you treat them good, they're yours for life. You've got to stroke them, make them feel you want them. Show them some passion.'

As if to punctuate my point, Paul Kelly, one of Sydney's principal suitors, crunches the Geelong full-back through his own posts for the first point of the second half. The crowd groans appreciatively.

'See what I mean, show you care by going that little bit further, giving that little bit extra.'

From a throw-in, Cresswell snares the loose ball and steers it home from 10 metres out.

'Don't waste opportunities to show your feelings,' I add as the Swans get a third quarter roll-on, their exploits fuelling my rhetoric.

Shannon Grant gets the ball on the 50 metre line, performs a League style dummy and sidesteps into space, sending the ball soaring for another six-pointer.

'Sneak your way into their affections by doing the unexpected with panache and grace.'

Now Maxfield is lining up for his third goal from 55 metres. The ball goes high but drops short. Plugger lunges through three defenders and the sigh is almost orgasmic, allowing me to stretch my metaphor even further.

'When it finally becomes time to perform don't go soft on them. Do it with vigour and commitment.'

Almost straight from the restart O'Loughlin gains possession in the centre square. Downfield it's Lockett again, wrestling with his luckless marker. The man who seduced Sydney is just too strong, and as he reaches skywards to meet the ball, the crowd cries like a satisfied lover.

'And most importantly, show you can give them a second dose of the same; and a third if they want it.'

Sydney continues its love dance into the final quarter, now 51 points up.

Lockett kicks his fifth goal after Kelly powers through the centre, busting two tackles before laying the ball on Plugger's tummy. Rocca follows up with his umpteenth behind of the day, again looking great in the air but lacking the finesse of his co-seducers.

Geelong, meanwhile, is going through the motions. God has moved onto the ball in a desperate bid to get the Cats attack moving, but all he does is make the Geelong forward line more aesthetically pleasing.

For the 44,000 Sydneysiders it has been the dream first date, the football equivalent of a limo ride to a five-star restaurant, fine wine, the best food, a show before some brandy by the fireplace back at your place. As the game winds down, the Swans provide the football equivalent of breakfast in bed the morning after, moving the ball across the SCG in fluid sweeps, as if to ask 'Was it good for you too?'

Kevin Dyson secures possession in defence, combining

with Luff and Maxfield to turn the attack around. Steaming across the centre, Dyson regathers possession and roosts the ball long to the Plugmeister. Lockett makes it six with a kick from an acute angle. Then it's O'Loughlin booting a long goal after Geelong kicks out on the full. Even the interchange players are showing themselves to be worthy suitors, Daniel McPherson kicking a long goal from 40 metres.

Geelong brings the winning margin back to 56 points by kicking the last four goals, but we excuse the Bloodstained Angels. After wooing us all afternoon they are entitled to rest easy.

POSTSCRIPT: The following night, rugby league's Monday Night Football kicks off. The authorities hail the full house as proof positive that the wounds are healing and people are coming back to the game. But gate receipts released later that week show that fewer than 10,000 fans have actually paid to see the game, the rest using their Big Mac vouchers. In contrast the Swans release figures showing about 30,000 payers, 14,000 members and solemn undertakings to make sure everyone fits into the ground for future games.

Third
Quarter

Plugger's Ton

Now we're in the run-in to the semi-finals and those Swan-nies just keep winning. The big question by round 19 is whether they'll stay in the top four, thus giving Sydney its first home final.

Since the Geelong game, the Swans had built their momentum, over-running the opposition with their well-drilled play, always geared at getting the ball to Plugger as quickly and cleanly as possible. They shut out St Kilda by 17 points in Melbourne, thanks to a 47-point third quarter. They avenge their first round 80-point thrashing at the hands of Adelaide with a 22-point win in front of 30,000 at home. Then they overwhelm Melbourne by 63 points at the SCG, emphasising their rising status in the competition by outplaying the struggling Demons across the paddock.

The only hiccup occurs in round 17 when they lose to Fre-mantle in Subiaco, ending an eight game winning streak. For the second time in 1996 the Dockers run Sydney ragged, out-pacing the Swans across the midfield with their distinctive ball in hand play. The result is a comprehensive 28-point defeat, but in context, the Swans are without an injured Lockett and had been heading for a defeat for several weeks. The consensus after the loss was that it was better to get the dud match out of the way now and refocus on the semis.

Through the winning streak Plugger had been rattling up his goal tally towards the magic 100. The century was the Mecca for all full-forwards, those most visible of AFL players. While it is true to say that the full-forwards live or die by the service from their team-mates, it is also true that once they make the mark they are the most exposed. When a full-forward misses a sitter there's nowhere to hide. Fans may easily forgive and forget the midfield intercept, the dropped mark, even the kick out on the full. But when one of their players misses from 30 metres in front, there is no forgetting. While the fans were harsh on failure, they also honoured success; no more so than when one of their own tallied up 100 in a season.

With 94 goals already under his belt, Plugger's impending ton was the main talking point in the lead-up to the Richmond game. Lockett was one of the few players in the League to regularly achieve the milestone. He had reached the magic three figures three times at St Kilda as well as in his first season for Sydney. This consistency put his talent in context. When Sydney had drafted him from St Kilda in 1995 he was one of the superstars of footy, the big-name star of a struggling side. Since coming to Sydney he had grown in stature, not only maintaining his personal performances, but inspiring another struggling team to take the step into the echelons of the elite clubs. That other players like Craig O'Brien would then follow him to Sydney on the back of his glowing references only underlined his value.

In return Sydney loved Plugger; the city had taken the bulky and boofy bloke under its wing, honouring his skills while respecting that it was media overkill which drove him from Victoria.

That Plugger carried his success with self-effacing understatement and the no-nonsense outlook that he was only doing his job made him all the more attractive to Sydney-siders. Despite its reputation as a garish and crass city, it was the quiet achievers like Plugger and the Waugh brothers rather than the glory boys and headline grabbers who commanded Sydney's ultimate respect.

The other thing about Plugger was his size. At 16 stone and six foot four he was a big lump of meat. This fitted Sydney's idea of a footy player. While the tight-shorted whippets like Kelly and Luff dominated the southern game, Sydneysiders were used to stars who carried a bit around the shoulders, a bit around the buttocks and a bit around the chin. Lockett resembled the tough guys of League, the dying breed of front-rowers being run out of town by the 10-metre rule. You could imagine him packing down with Blocker Roach and Fatty Vautin. He may play a foreign game and come from a foreign State but Plugger looked like a Sydney footballer.

For all these reasons, all eyes were on Lockett as the Swans saunter onto the SCG on a sunny August afternoon. Richmond, just clinging to the top eight, assign a tall mid-fielder, Paul Bulluss to play on Lockett. Jostling our hero before play has even started, Bulluss immediately earmarks himself as the subject of today's heckle.

The heckle is one of the pure joys of live football. By getting a seat close to the action fans can actually interact with opposing players, challenging them to retain their composure in the face of deprecating commentary of their ability, physique and/or lineage. If the target is carefully chosen and the execution is carried out shrewdly, heckling can have a tangible impact on the match. My fondest memory is of St George winger Ian Herron making a total mess of a high ball in the face of constant taunts of 'cheer up Herron!' from a tight-knit heckling circle under the fig tree at Bear Park. As he slunk off to the reserves bench we knew we'd played our little part in his demise.

When the heckle is really working it ceases to be a one-sided exchange, an isolated ranting from a one-eyed hood. Instead the tirade takes on a life of its own, entire sections of the crowd taking up the call as the hapless recipient of the abuse attempts to retain focus. And so it was with Paul Bulluss. From the second he starts jostling our Tony pre-bounce, the group in front of the Noble Stand don't let up. 'Who are you, Bulluss?' Juzzo screams. 'We need details of your genealogy for our scientific study of losers!'

Sydney is looking for Lockett from the opening seconds. Cresswell, sporting a hairstyle that can only be described as the anti-Mullet (the old pudding bowl look) sizes him up but the ball drops short, that man Bulluss clearing it down-field. But when Roos intercepts and relays the ball back to Grant, Lockett has swung across the circle into space while Bulluss is still recovering from his ill-directed clearing kick. Lockett lays back and drills the ball home from 40 metres and his tally has reached 95 within sixty seconds. Bulluss stands hunched, head bowed in his black and gold strip which carries the anti-alcohol message 'Drink, Drive, Bloody Idiot'.

'At least the second line is accurate, Bulluss,' Juzzo roars.

The ball moves crisply through the centre, safe handballs allowing the Swans midfield to run through the mark. Maxfield, Grant and Kelly combine, before the skipper sends the ball wide into the attacking zone. Troy Luff, one of those players who performs way above the sum of his parts, launches into a full-length dive and swallows the pill. Eddie waves his 'Luff is in the Air' sign as Luff, recently liberated from his Ted Mulray hairdo, threads the ball through from 45.

'Where were you, Bulluss? Marking your shadow?' Juzzo again, at his cryptic best.

Bulluss' life is not getting any better. Luff takes another mark before combining with the midfield kings, Maxfield and Kelly. Again Kelly puts the ball deep into the goal square and Plugger lunges high, leaving Bulluss grasping for air.

'If you were a bunny you couldn't even catch the calicivirus, Bulluss,' Juzzo screeches as Lockett kicks number 96 from a tight angle, first thinking it through then kicking it through.

Luff, dominating the right flank, wins another possession marking strongly. He centres to Seymour, running across the edge of the attacking circle before off-loading to Scott Direen, a player normally found deep in defence. Direen steadies, then picks out Plugger who's surprised absolutely no-one by shrugging off Bulluss like the mild irritant that he is. The roar goes up around the SCG as Lockett kicks his third, but we're screaming for the real hero of the afternoon: 'BULL-USS, BULL-USS, BULL-USS.'

It's not an aggressive attack on the hapless Tiger, merely the beauty of a well-directed heckle. The fact the poor bugger is being munched mercilessly by Plugger just adds to the theatre. We're singing his name again when Lockett casually nudges him out of the square to ensure a clear grab at another Kelly drop-punt and set up his fourth goal of the quarter right on the siren.

It's almost a merciful relief when Bulluss is moved off Lockett in the second quarter. With the quarter-time score already 32–8, you get the feeling there would be no contest at all if the Tigers persisted with the stratagem.

Richmond actually kicks the first goal of the second term, although Sydney replies immediately as Lockett registers goal number 99, reaching high for a reefing long ball from Hueskes. The crowd waits expectantly for Plugger's ton but it's Richmond which starts blazing away, kicking a long-bouncing goal and following it up with a 50 metre thump to bring the margin back to two goals.

We think Plugger has his shot at 100 when he grabs a

Maxfield kick well inside kicking range. But the umpire fouls our hero for no apparent reason and we howl at the injustice. But the Richmond comeback has shifted the focus away from the milestone and back to the contest; and when Tiger midfielder Merendera hoists the ball from 55 metres, there's just one goal in it.

Faced with the Richmond resurgence, the Swans do what they have all season, they step up a gear right across the park. Like a well-oiled machine they work the ball out of defence: Direen kicks long to Dunkley, who can't mark it, but manages to gain sufficient control to scoop it to McPherson, who chips to the edge of the centre square. This time O'Loughlin lunges, but again misses the mark. Richmond gets a touch, but it's Cresswell bursting through the centre who gets the vital tap, nudging the ball across to Garlick. He handballs crisply back to O'Loughlin who, seeing no-one in front of him, drops the ball onto his boot and watches it wobble through at a low trajectory. The length of the field movement hasn't been your copybook kick and mark affair, it's been more of the hustle and the rumble. Without actually securing possession, the Swans midfielders have controlled it, setting up the inexorable surge that has led to six points.

Straight from the restart Kelly grabs the ball out of the ruck and thumps a handball downfield. Luff taps it onto Grant, sprinting through the centre, seeing Lockett in space and picking him out with one of his signature deliveries, smooth and assured.

The roar builds around the ground as Plugger sets for his hundredth goal of 1996. The kick is from 35 metres, pretty much straight in front. He goes through his socks and jocks routine, picks up the Sherrin and takes nine deliberate steps before giving it his signature whack. The ball sails high as the crowd flocks onto the field, almost mobbing the goal umpire as he signals the auspicious moment.

They come onto the ground in waves, giving expression

144

to the seasons of frustration at being forbidden access onto the hallowed turf by jumped-up security guards. The invasion to celebrate 100 goals is a tradition that not even the SCG Trust can control. There are simply too many spectators to arrest. Instead the yellow-jacketed security guards grope around like speed-addled nightclub bouncers, looking for an order to restore; indiscriminately grabbing the invaders and ordering them off. It's not fair: they have much more fun when it's just one spectator they can crash tackle into the boundary fence.

Meanwhile, Plugger is totally surrounded by photographers, desperately trying to snap tomorrow's front page photo. Then the security leeches turn their attention to the press and try to disperse that crowd. You've got these concentric circles that have developed around Plugger: the cameras, then the security thugs, then the field invaders, then the rest of us who are all standing in our seats giving the big man a standing ovation as we take in these crazy, quasi-religious scenes.

It takes at least five minutes to clear the field, the outpouring of euphoria mixed with a healthy anarchy that has been stifled all year. No-one is hurt, no-one is offended, the crowd run on and cheer Plugger's achievement, while the Tigers huddle defensively midfield. But the disruption has ended the Sydney run-on and it's Richmond who snaps an easy goal to bring the margin back to two straight kicks.

Mark Bayes, the Swans' longest serving player who's been on the injured list all season, finally sprints onto the ground. The old-timers rave about the tall blond defender, and I soon discover why as he reaches high for a mark on the 50, Lockett leads and stretches to grab the ball, marking 40 metres from goal. He kicks his seventh straight and we're wondering how many today?

From the restart Kelly and Maxfield execute the perfect

touches to clear and it's Bayes again, tapping the ball to O'Loughlin, then running around him as the dark-skinned midfielder mesmerises three Tiger defenders by weaving and dummying like a rubber man. Bayes is fed the ball in space and kicks it long and low for another six-pointer. The man who is rated in most all-time Top Ten Sydney lists is back and the cheers of Eddie tell me this will be a plus in the finals.

The Swans fans continue their celebrations as the protagonists go to the long break. We talk about Plugger and the importance of heroes.

One of the most shocking things I've ever read was the survey that found Michael Jordan was the most popular sports star amongst Australian teenagers. The story caught me by surprise; I'd presumed the nation's youth still followed cricket and rugby, not some American game played by genetic freaks.

'The problem is that none of these kids will ever grow up to be a seven-foot Negro playing in the NBA,' I pronounce. 'And it's not about race, it's about reality. We're talking sport which is once-removed from reality, the kids have no hope of ever achieving what their heroes have.'

'What about Shane Heal,' Juzzo asks. 'The little blond guy who's made it to the NBA?'

'Sure, but I'd argue that Heal's the exception that proves the rule. He's just one out of all the thousands of little blond Aussies dreaming of bouncing balls with Jordan and Shaq. Compare it with cricket, for instance. Anyone can grow up to be a cranky little batsman who bowls offies and captains his country. You don't need to be at the end of a line of genetic impurities to keep wickets, just concentration and a good eye. It's just more attainable.

'It's the same with footy. There's all sizes out there today from Filandia to Plugger—there's no restrictions. It puts Rules ahead of rugby league, where you need to be built like a box, and it puts it above basketball where height is everything.

'But the heroes are the vital factors; the Shane Warnes who inspire kids to take up leg-spin, the Greg Normans for golf, Pat Cashes for tennis and of course the Pluggers.'

We toast the big man as the Swans run out for the second term. He's straight into the action, way too big for hapless defender number three as he kicks goal number nine.

'The other thing about local heroes is that they are going to be vital in keeping our Australian culture going,' I rave on, as Richmond peg one back.

'How so?'

'Basketball is pure America, it's Coca-Cola, it's Mc-Donald's, it's back to the front baseball caps and drive-by murders. You may see no link there, but they are all part of the same continuum. Basketball is just another slice of the US of A being spread around the world like any other commodity. It's little more than a commercial exercise in expansion. It grows through private consortia who import the players, the mascots, the razzamatazz. Basketball lacks a soul because it has been developed to make a profit. It has no organic connection to the societies, all around the world, where it is taking root like a cancer.

'At least our local games like footy and cricket still mean something to us as Australians. And Aussie Rules, more than any other game can help us survive this Americanisation of our culture. The beautiful thing about Rules is that it can't grow bigger, it is a national, not an international, game. Therefore it will always be constrained by Australia's borders. There can be no attempt to Super League it too, because no-one else is bloody interested.

'In this way blokes like Plugger could just be the saviours of Australian culture.'

My monologue is broken by another Sydney goal. Bayes kicks his second from a sharp angle. Then it's the little weedy bloke with frizzy hair and a pigtail running through the middle of the field. His name is Clinton King and he looks like he should be at day care rather than in the middle of the SCG.

'You see, if a little guy like that can play Firsts, anyone can!'

Lockett kicks his first behind just before three-quarter time, but the fans are now forgiving.

Sydney still looks vulnerable at three-quarter time and when the Tigers kick the first goal of the last term, they're back to within 11 points. But from there, the Swans run away with it, booting eight goals in the last quarter.

Kelly finds Plugger's chest with a sharp delivery for goal number nine. Then the meister outmuscles another marker, tapping the ball up once, twice, three times, before grabbing the mark casually under his wing to set up number 10. Kickett pops up with a six-pointer and then Bayes kicks his third. The Richmond challenge has been clinically defused and the Swans are scoring at will.

As the 30,000 Sydneysiders rise to cheer Plugger's eleventh, again after service from Kelly, I sense the importance of their success. The Swans are filling a missing link for Aussie Rules, forging a stronghold in virgin territory. The challenge is even greater than in Brisbane where there has always been a strong Rules presence. With Sydney, the AFL is a national competition and Australia has a national game, which is not interested in spreading the word into Asia or America through Foxtel or Optus. Just a sport that is fun to watch and, when you're up by seven goals in the fourth quarter, fun to play as well.

Kelly is rewarded for setting up goals all afternoon with one of his own, after a 25 metre dash into an open goal. Then it's Dyson, linking Dunkley to Lockett with a mighty hoik. Plugger's kicked his 12. It's only left to Mark Bayes now, to kick his fourth and let Sydney's newcomers know he's back in business.

The final quarter blow-out has red and white flags waving around the ground, but at the end of the day it's one man, Tony Lockett, who showed us something special. It's something that ruined Paul Bulluss' afternoon, neutered the crowd Nazis and reawakened my hope for Australian culture. It was no small feat from a man with no small feet.

The Players Swans Love to Hate

By far the most enjoyable sideshow at the footy is the heckle. Personal abuse of players take two central forms: hopeful deprecation of the opposing stars and cruel ridicule of the also-rans. Special targets for Swans fans are the players who have the dubious privilege of marking Plugger. While the content of the heckle is often spiteful and deeply personal, opposing fans will happily acknowledge an intelligent insult and respond in kind.

PAUL BULLUSS (Richmond): Incompetent Tiger utility, performs equally poorly in any position. Easily distracted by hecklers.

JAMES HIRD (Essendon): Self-assured mummy's boy who wears long sleeves to hide gravel rash. Unparalleled ability to take marks and kick goals makes him all the more irritating.

STEPHEN KERNAHAN (Carlton): The League's premier Mullet

cut, whose ungainly lope betrays years in the saddle. The derided figurehead of one of Melbourne's most hated teams.

GARY ABLETT (Geelong): Known as God in Geelong, but there are no believers in Sydney after his woeful 1996. Balding, aging has-been whose skills are fading faster than his looks.

WAYNE CAREY (North Melbourne): Smug and surly New Age Guy whose mouth gets him into more trouble off the field than on. Suspected of shaving his armpits for 1996 grand final.

ROGER MERRETT (Brisbane): Ugliest man in the League who easily adapted to Brisbane's red-neck lifestyle.

BEN COUSINS (West Coast): Blow-waved idiot savant whose 1996 season will, with justice, prove to be a flash in the pan.

THE JARMANS (Adelaide): Barossa-based clan of crew-cutted Aryan thugs who are believed to be the product of genetic experimentation.

JOHN PLATTEN (Hawthorn): Middle-aged hippy sponsored by Joico; suspected of taking magic mud cake as a performance enhancing drug.

Plugger Unplugged

Tony Lockett was the Sydney Swans in 1996. There was a myriad of reasons why Plugger set Sydney alight: he came to Sydney with the rebel reputation, he was one of the AFL's all-time greats already, he even looked like our version of a footy player. But most importantly, Plugger was the best at what he did. He could catch a footy and kick it straight. And, perhaps surprisingly, there was a further dimension. For beneath the furrowed brow and footy cliches lurked a philosopher: a bloke who's good at footy, but doesn't believe that makes him better than anyone else. Someone who prefers privacy to public adulation and can't help wondering what all the fuss is about.

Where did you come from? We know you've been in Sydney for two years, but what happened before that?

I was born and bred in Ballarat, about 120 kilometres west of Melbourne and played footy with North Ballarat from the age of seven. I played in the under-12s when I was seven and played right through till the summer of 1982 when I went down to St Kilda at the age of sixteen.

So were you a star from the moment you ran out on the field?

No, I don't think I got any kicks when I was a seven year old playing under-12s, I was just there because there were no under-8s or under-10s. I think I played in the forward pocket, but I don't remember too much about those days. You just made the progression as you got a bit older and a bit stronger and a bit taller.

Did you always want to be a forward kicking goals?

I don't know, you just played anywhere as a kid. All you wanted to do was kick the footy. I never played in the backline in all my life, I was always on the ball or on the forward line.

So when did you realise you were pretty good at footy?

I don't know if I ever got the idea I was pretty good at footy, it's a hard question really, things just happen I guess. I certainly think there were kids who were better than me in my age group.

Any of them go anywhere?

None of them established long League careers, although I think a few were invited to train down in Melbourne. I guess I might have just been a little bit lucky, I suppose.

What got you to St Kilda?

Back in those days there was no draft, they had zones. Each club had a zone in the bush and Ballarat was in St Kilda's zone so any player that came from Ballarat had to play for St Kilda. No ifs, no buts. They had a development officer in

Ballarat and they had two squads—under-15s and under-17s. I must have been about fourteen when I got invited to train with them. We'd train on a Sunday morning and we'd have a camp about twice a year. The Ballarat squad, the Frankston squad and a city squad would all come together and play matches against each other. You got introduced to St Kilda through that junior development squad. You'd go from there to under-19s and then to seniors.

Was everyone in Ballarat a St Kilda fan?

Not all of them were fans, but a lot of people followed the Ballarat boys through their careers with St Kilda. St Kilda was everyone's second side if you know what I mean. If you didn't barrack for St Kilda, you had a bit of a soft spot for them because all the local boys went down and played with them.

Do you remember any particular game when you got picked out by the selectors?

When all the squads met for the games down in Melbourne in under-17s, I got player of the carnival. Over the three games I got nominated as player of the meet. So I guess after that I was always earmarked for later in life if my footy progressed further on.

So what about coming to Melbourne? As a sixteen year old you came down to St Kilda; did they keep you in school or were you left to your own devices?

I tried a couple of jobs. I started off in a nursery, I worked at the footy ground for a while, just sort of odds and ends. But all I really wanted to do was play footy.

I read somewhere that your first job was as a greyhound catcher.

That was before footy at the Ballarat dog track. That was just as a kid, a thirteen or fourteen year old, it was just what the kids used to do, grab the dogs after the race was over.

And what about the footy at St Kilda?

Well, I came down in the summer of '82, trained all summer and played in reserves straight away. I never played in the under-19s.

How did you find the change?

Oh, it was very hard. I'd come out of a year of under-16s, playing against kids my own size or smaller. All of a sudden you're playing against men and obviously much better footballers. So the change was very hard, but one you had to adapt to.

Have you built yourself up a lot since then? Were you a big kid?

No, only just your average size until I was seventeen or eighteen, I suppose. I just got bigger since then.

St Kilda were the duds of the League weren't they?

Yeah, they struggled. My first three years at St Kilda we had the wooden spoon. The whole three years. The early days were pretty hard and tough and not that enjoyable.

One of the things Sydney people remember from when you were at St Kilda was the match against Sydney when you got suspended for clobbering Peter Caven. What happened there?

That was just an incident on the ground. It was just one of those things where St Kilda was down 40 or 50 points in the last quarter and we came back and won. People were looking for a reason, looking for an incident to pick on and they picked that one. There are plenty of worse things that happen in the course of a game.

When you came up to Sydney did you think that incident would be a hard part of the move?

I don't know about hard, but I thought that there would be some ramifications from it. But I came up here and trained hard and we've had a couple of good seasons, the club's going terrific and that's a forgotten incident now.

What was the feeling at the club like when you came up? They'd been on a really long losing streak, was there the feeling that there might be a decent football team somewhere here?

I think that started last year. We had a couple of good recruits, with a heap of real good young kids who they pulled out of the draft. We went from being a very ordinary side to a side that was quite competitive last year. Instead of taking one step again in 1996, I think we took three or four.

Have you thought much about what changed last season?

I just think the young kids got better, they worked harder, they improved from being seventeen year olds to eighteen year olds. I just think we played a lot harder and everyone just enjoyed it much more and they played on a high for most of the year.

Some of those games where there was a full house and the game was close, did you pick up the energy out there from the crowd?

For sure. You've got 30,000 or 40,000 people out there

screaming and yelling and carrying on. Certainly you forget about how tired you are. A few years ago the crowds were very low, but last season you could hardly get a seat. It was just fantastic.

Did you notice a turnaround during the year?

Geelong was definitely the turnaround game. It was a full house and we put on a good performance. People could finally see we were worth going and watching.

Why did you make the decision to come up to Sydney?

I just thought I needed a change after twelve years with St Kilda. They were very enjoyable years, but towards the end my footy was suffering a bit. I didn't have the passion I should have had and it was time for a change. I offered to go to Richmond first.

Was that because they had first choice in the draft?

I'm not sure how it worked out with that. But I thought Richmond would be a good side to go to. But as it worked out I ended up coming to Sydney and not only has it been a change of club, it's been a change of home, change of State. The whole lot's changed and honestly it's been probably the best move of my life.

What do you like about living up here?

For a start the weather's that much better than Melbourne. You don't really get a chance to appreciate it unless you've lived down south. I don't know, it's just not quite so fanatical and crazy here. I mean, they obviously love winners up here in Sydney, but every day in Melbourne the papers are just full of football and it's just constant pressure on you the whole time. You just get sick of it after a while.

Although it was almost like that in Sydney at the end of the season.

But the end of the year up here is what it's like down there all year round. Through the summer and everything. You just can't be on that pinnacle all the time. You've got to come down and get away from it for a while. Then you can come back up to it, I guess. I don't know, they're just a very fanatical State—they just love their footy.

You chose to live down in the southern suburbs of Sydney. Are you down by the beach?

I'm down towards Wollongong. I just knew a family who lived there, so that just made things a little bit easier for us.

One of the moments I remember most this year was when you kicked the 100 goals against Richmond and everyone ran onto the field. That's a bit of a tradition in Melbourne isn't it?

Yeah, that's been going on for years now.

How did you feel when you kicked it?

It's a terrific feeling. It's what every full-forward sets out to achieve and if you can kick 100 goals it's a great achievement.

Do you remember actual incidents from games or is it all a bit of a blur?

Most of it's a blur.

What about the kick to win the final against Essendon?

Oh, you remember those kicks for the rest of your life. There's been so much emphasis on it and it's been replayed in your mind again and again and again.

Does it seem the same on TV as it seems in your mind?

I've seen it a couple of times on TV and that's about it. But I mean, it doesn't really matter how you do it, it's the result that matters, isn't it? It was lucky enough to go through and we were lucky enough to win.

You ended up with the most discussed groin in Australia. How bad were you injury-wise in those last couple of games?

I've had four operations since the end of the season. I'm no surgeon, so I can't tell you the terminology, but the surgeon thought it was pretty severe, whatever it was. I just have to rest now and get it back to working order again.

How many metres did the injury take off your kicking game?

It's hard to say. If you could see the way I was kicking at training, you'd say it had taken a lot off. But to look at that kick against Essendon, it was probably a 55 or 60 metre kick and you wouldn't think you'd lost anything. It's just different situations. One you're at training and there's no adrenalin, you get to the last game when it means you're going to be playing in a grand final. Humans can do amazing things when the adrenalin's going. I can honestly say that I didn't even think about my knee or my groin when I was going for that kick.

You'd had a few pain-killing needles as well?

Yeah.

Not much feeling downstairs?

Not a great deal, no.

I guess the other thing that intrigues people who are new to the game is what's actually going on in the forward pocket? What distinguishes the good full-forward from the average one?

There's that many different things to be a good player in any position. A lot of things you can't train for, a lot are instinctive because the ball's going to come to you in a hundred different ways—it'll come to you rushed, or low along the ground or kicked high. Blokes with pressure on them deliver the ball differently to when there's no pressure. I'd say it's mainly instinctive and you just have to take your own initiative to try and be in front as much as you can and put yourself in the best position for your team-mate to kick the ball to you. Don't make it too hard for him; lead to where it's going to be easy to kick the ball to you.

Is there a zone you're trying to get into?

There's not always space. Full-forwards just rely so much on the blokes up field. We only really put the icing on the cake. It's a glorified position.

What about the kicking? How much work would you put in?

I've put a lot of time in over the years. Obviously, your job is to kick the goals and if you're a bad kick you shouldn't be there in the first place. There's a bit of pressure on you. If you get ten shots at goal, ideally at worst you should be able to kick seven–three. Given that it's not wet conditions or the wind howling a hundred mile an hour, that makes it difficult for everyone. But on a normal sort of day, it would be a bad day if I didn't convert at least seven of those ten shots for goal. I'd be disappointed if I didn't.

It's one of those positions as well, where you're the one that out there, they'll remember your mistakes.

I guess so, but as I said before, it's a glorified position. A bloke can have twenty kicks and ten handballs in the middle of the ground and people say he's played good. A full-forward can get eight kicks and kick eight goals and get more praise for it. It's a bit silly really. As I say, it's glorified and just because you kick the goals you get a bit more adulation and praise when there's a lot of blokes up the ground doing a lot harder work than what you're doing.

What about your future with the Swans?

I've got two more years to go and then there's an option of two more after that. I don't want to say now whether I'm going to be playing that long, but I'm definitely aiming at that and I don't see any reason why I shouldn't be playing that long.

And what do you think about life after football? Are you going to go back to Victoria?

No. I'm going to stay up here in Sydney.

And do you think Sydney will continue supporting the Swans after the '96 season?

I think it's going to depend on the success we have, but I would like to think that people will support right through.

161

I think we've won our supporters, now we just have to maintain them. I think that with the way the club's structured now, the administration and the people they have working around in the club is second to none and there's no reason why the club won't continue to be run professionally. The days are long gone now when players didn't want to come and play for Sydney. All of a sudden, there's a lot of interest from the players and that's a very good sign for the future.

Ramblings of a Footy Chick

Edwina Throsby

A boy I know was pretty upset to discover he had contracted herpes from an unfortunate but remarkably enjoyable fling he had with a girl who worked for a major city financial institution. It's amazing, he told me about two weeks later, when you get this disease yourself, it's like you are initiated into a secret club. All these people who you've known for years tell you that they have it too.

While I don't want to compare our great national sport to a venereal disease, when I discovered Aussie Rules at the end of the 1995 season, much the same thing happened to me.

But let me go back.

I was born in Sydney. In summer my father watched Test cricket with tedious enthusiasm. When my family sat in the traffic on the way home from the beach, we weren't allowed to talk so my father could listen to Alan McGilvray on the car radio detailing the annihilation of the English team. In winter, when we would visit my grandmother, Dad would slow the car down to a crawl as we passed North Sydney Oval so he could wind down the window and yell 'Up the Mighty Bears!'

I left school, went to uni and got a job pulling beers in the local pub. On Sunday evenings at 6.30 the races would end and the rugby league match of the day would be turned on the four TV screens that hung over the bar. One week some blow-in was stupid enough to come in a good hour before the match was due to be televised and announce that the Dragons had flogged Souths. In the ensuing fracas I can't quite remember who actually threw him out onto the street in a frenzy of abuse, but I think it was the publican whose father had been a Rabbitoh in the 1940s. I never saw him again.

Needless to say, I quickly learned that I had two choices. I could learn to like rugby league or I could resign. Poverty dictated that only the first option was viable, so, with an adaptability that surprised even me, I found myself behind the bar in a red and green sweater screaming like a groupie at the telly. One thing led to another and soon I was hosting State of Origin parties where everyone on the street bought their TV over (the record was twelve, all going at once). I threw on a bucket of prawns, party pies, footy franks and a case of beer and wept when Laurie Daley fumbled the ball and jeered in the face of my Queensland-born flatmate when Mal Meninga did the same thing.

I was a league chick, well and truly.

It's hard to isolate the genesis of my conversion. I think the Great Boot Wearer in the Sky caused many factors to converge at the same time. For a start, I graduated from uni and left the pub. My Queensland flatmate fell in love with a boy in a red convertible and moved out, depriving me of my main rival. Cowley and Arko began that unpleasant business and their inability to reach a resolution took the fun right out of State of Origin. The Rabbitohs got maybe five tries in the entire season.

And then, one golden day in the late winter of 1995, a friend of mine up from Melbourne took me to see the Swans play Essendon at the SCG. I discovered an Eden, where the consumption of beer and yelling of obscenities was not only tolerated, it was almost compulsory. As the Swans played towards an upset win, I heard pan flute music drifting over the Randwick end. A golden light shimmered off the players' chiselled shoulders as they ran in slow motion over the lush green grass, past the unicorns and griffins which had cascaded down the Doug Walters Stand to preen themselves along the 50 metre line. When the final siren blew it was a call from God and I joined the beautiful people who stripped off their earthly clothes and ran onto the field. I leapt onto the back of a nearby Pegasus, who obligingly flew me home.

I can't remember going to bed that night. I do remember waking up the next morning, somehow dressed in a red and white crocheted travel rug and a Plugger beanie, realising that finally, after twenty-something years of aimlessness, I Had Found My True Path.

Summer was eternity. My Essendon-supporting mate returned to Melbourne leaving me heart-broken and alone in a sea of rugby league-following footy heathens. Or so I thought.

At the beginning of the 1996 season, I gathered together my scarf and thermos and skulked down to the SCG to see my Messiahs. And there was Jo. And Carmel. And Peter, and little Jo, and Darren, and Rachel, and Sean, and Carolyn and Jenny and Ashley and Ashley's dad, who used to play for South Melbourne. And they were all drinking beer and screaming obscenities.

I went to barbies and friends who I'd known since school were saying, 'How about those Swannies, eh?' And while I was unsure about their STD status, I knew one thing—I had uncovered a secret society that was Not Going To Be Secret Any More, that we were prepared to walk down the street Lifting That Noble Banner High, Cheer Cheering, Onward to Victory.

Mergers and Acquisitions

As the season has unfolded one of the most striking aspects of the Swans' resurgence has been the huge numbers of fans clad in red and white turning up at the Melbourne games. You can see them on the telly replays—older-looking fans in washed-out jumpers and beanies; more likely to have the traditional red V than the Opera House logo; more likely to cheer for 'South' than 'Sydney'. These are the dispossessed; the South Melbourne fans who lost a club when the Swans moved north.

As the season progresses, there appears to be more and more of these retro-fans huddled in the stands at bleak Melbourne grounds. At a few games, notably St Kilda at Football Park, they actually seem to outnumber the home side, welcoming the Bloodstained Angels resurgence like a loved one who's just returned from travelling the world. Fourteen years after moving to Sydney, the Swans have come home.

When I score a mid-week trip to Melbourne for work I can't resist taking a couple of hours to visit the Swans' old home. I jump in one of Jeff Kennett's crisp, clean cabs and ask the uniformed driver to take me to South Melbourne.

'Whereabouts?' he asks. 'Most of it's just freeway and factories.'

'The old South Melbourne ground—the Lake Oval,' I grapple with my ignorance.

Over the Yarra we drive, on the road to St Kilda where people roller-blade down the esplanade on weekends. Over ring roads and past leafy esplanades we drive, through Albert Park and Middle Park; now middle-class suburbs set on the edge of the Port Melbourne docks in the shadow of the Crown Casino. The cityscape changes with every block, switching from affluent to bland and back again. The area reminds me of Sydney's Alexandria; a mixture of ugly factories and offices and old working-class homes, quavering on the brink of a home renovator invasion—all watched over by two giant Housing Commission blocks.

We approach Albert Park and the cabbie points across the way. 'There's your Lake Oval, right in the middle of the Grand Prix track.'

I get out and wander across the park. It's hard to imagine this calm mass of green as the home for rev-heads and their beautiful hangers-on; the prize Jeff stole from Adelaide. The Grand Prix is an international event run annually through the city streets, an event with as much soul and social utility as a casino, but an integral part of Kennett's gaming economy. The park is dotted with slick new complexes; a huge gym and aquatic centre part of the blueprint for Melbourne's bid for the 2006 Commonwealth Games.

In the middle of this symbol of 1990s development sits the old Lake Oval, although these days it's named after a tyre maker and is home to the South Melbourne soccer club. Bob Jane Stadium: the name doesn't quite fit with the old ground. I wander through an open gate and around the fence. There's a couple of stands which look like they were built in the early 1900s, not dissimilar to the old stands at Bear Park that were relocated from the SCG. There's still a ring of benches around the outfield and banks of grass. I close my eyes and think of Bob Pratt and the Chimp, imagining the crush of a full house on match day, as the Swans battle through another season.

I hear shouts from across the field and a bunch of guys jog out doing tricks with a soccer ball. The magic is broken. I take my leave and wander onto Clarendon Street looking for refreshment.

A pub, the Cricket Club Hotel looms invitingly; not one of the yuppified glass and chrome numbers, but a real pub, with a bar trough and dartboard in the corner. I sidle up to the bar, get the language right and order a pot. I look around the bar and notice that it's decked out in Swans memorabilia, from faded photos of successful sides in the past right through to images of Plugger.

I turn to the old-timer next to me at the bar. 'Still keeping the faith?'

'Yeah,' he replies. 'It's been a while but the wounds have finally started to heal.'

As we sip our beers we talk about the 1996 season, I confess I'm a newcomer and discover he's been watching the Swans since he was a kid.

'So what went down in the early '80s,' I ask, hungry for insight into the relocation.

'It was really a case of a few things happening at once. For one, the VFL had always wanted to expand the competition nationally and the idea of a team in Sydney was obviously part of that. They actually brought a NSW team into the Escort pre-season Cup in 1980. At one stage there had been a push to move Fitzroy up there and I think Carlton had played a few exhibition games there too. But the VFL was still very much a suburban comp and no-one wanted to leave their base.

'What happened with the Swans, though, was that they were really struggling. They had been for years, making the finals just once since the 1945 grand final. By the early eighties membership had fallen to less than 2,000, debts were mounting and our home ground was in urgent need of renovation. From what I understand, the South committee did its sums, realised they didn't add up and decided they had two options: either relocate or wind the whole show up.'

'How did that go down with the fans?' I ask, ordering another round.

'All hell broke loose! A Keep South At South committee was formed when word of the move leaked out in 1981. There were rallies at Lake Oval after the games, fundraising drives, public meetings. It was theft and this was war. Those behind the move were branded traitors and a lot of longstanding friendships fell by the wayside. Don't forget, it was people's lives we were talking about; it was a very emotional time.'

'So what decided the issue?'

'I think in the end, they gave the dissidents access to the books. When they realised how bad the figures really were the resistance just sort of collapsed.

'Once the Swans moved north there was a lot of grieving—like a death in the family. But we still had Ricky Quade and Barry Round and we all cheered when they won the Escort Cup at the start of 1982. In those first couple of years a lot of us still turned up to Swans' away games.

'The real break came in the mid 1980s when Edelsten came on the scene. It was like he was prostituting footy with the showbiz side of it. That's when the Swans stopped being our side, there was no link with South Melbourne any more—it was basically embarrassing to watch all the carry-on.'

'So the Swanettes didn't do it for you?'

'That might be fine at a circus, but this was footy. The other thing that was happening about that time was the further expansion of the competition—to Brisbane and

Perth. As the competition expanded, there were fewer games that the Swans were playing in Victoria and the interest obviously started to wane because of that. By the end of the '80s I was cheering for them on the telly games, but that real passion, the fire in the belly, was starting to go out.

'The funny thing is that it took that atrocious losing streak through the early 1990s for things to really turn around. By mid-1993 there was serious talk about the Sydney Swans dying and the whole issue was out there again: extinction. I think at that point a lot of the old South fans realised they still wanted to see the red and whites playing footy, even if they were called Sydney and didn't play in Melbourne very often.

'The other thing was that we related to the losing Swans much more than the Edelsten version. We were battlers again, like we'd always been, bar a few notable years. More so, when the Swans started turning the corner in 1995 and then playing with such passion and success this year, it was the resurgence that the South fans had been waiting for since 1945. Just because the team called Sydney home, didn't mean we weren't going to enjoy it!'

'What about the new Sydney fans like me, how do you feel about us?'

'Well, when you're buying the beers we'll put up with you. But seriously, you've got to accept a degree of scepticism on our part. Like where have you been for the last fourteen years? For us it just goes to show that Sydney is a shallow place that only loves winners.'

'True, it's been a bit of a bandwagon thing, but remember we always had League in the past.'

'Granted, I suppose it's been a bit like us in 1982, only you folk lost your whole game. But there was another side to it I was going to mention. I have no doubt that the full houses at the SCG this year have spurred the Swans on to performances that would have been impossible if they were playing in front of a couple of thousand. The support, for whatever reason, has helped the Swans immensely and for that, I suppose you've got our begrudging thanks.'

We toast each other, realising we are opposite sides to the Swans coin.

'It's strange sitting in a bar like this,' I confess. 'It really underlines the fact that the Swans are a two-city side. You have the love of the nation's biggest city and, at the same time, you have a real sense of history being maintained by the old South brigade.

'If we in Sydney understand the history, it will help guard against the excesses of another Edelsten. From what I can gather, everyone treated it as a party, rather than part of a cultural tradition, so they had no qualms about walking away when the music stopped. Learning about the Blood-stained Angels is the best way to develop a solid Sydney base.'

'Never underestimate the history,' my comrade agrees. 'As you become more familiar with the game you'll get a feel for the reverence of it.'

'A bit like cricket—the rich history of WG Grace, Body-line and Bradman.'

'Exactly. A base from which next week's match derives its real meaning.'

The news comes on the TV and it leads with the proposed Melbourne–Hawthorn merger. It's one of a range of similar proposals that have been raised this season: North with Fitzroy, Fitzroy with Brisbane, St Kilda with anyone who will have them.

In what seems like a rerun of 1982 there are passionate public protests from both sides. The deal looks like being scotched by a Jewish businessman who confesses to knowing nothing about the game but wants to bankroll Melbourne. Meanwhile, past Hawthorn stars are berating the move, arguing a merger will kill both clubs.

171

The mergers were being actively promoted by the AFL, which was offering big financial incentives for the Melbourne teams to merge or relocate, conscious of the way rugby league had ripped itself apart for failing to go down this path.

'History repeating itself?'

'Watching these mergers I can't help thinking the Swans were probably lucky,' my drinking partner replies. 'If you merge two local sides I think you really do lose the identity—I mean, what do you call them: the Demon-Hawks?'

'Maybe just the Dorks,' I suggest.

'I think the one team who got it right was Fitzroy. Sure they're moving to Brisbane, but they're taking their colours, emblem, history and identity with them. Unlike when we went to Sydney, there's already a strong club there with good players and a loyal support base. For the Fitzroy fans they'll still be cheering for the Lions on the television every weekend and they'll still have a chance to go to the Melbourne games. It's not so much a case of losing a team but gaining a realistic chance of a finals appearance.

'They've learnt the lesson of the Swans: if you relocate intelligently you can keep a support base in two cities and make the club even stronger.'

'It's a lesson that League could have learnt too,' I agree. 'They've set up new teams around the country, even across to New Zealand, without a thought to rationalising the local sides. If only they'd bitten the bullet in the early 1980s and moved—say St George to Illawarra or Newtown, who eventually died, to Canberra—they could have kept their Sydney fans while maintaining a viable comp.'

Easy to map out history in hindsight we agree, just thankful that the Swans had lucked in and got it right. We consummate our newfound camaraderie with one last pot.

'See you at the MCG on grand final day,' he shakes my

hand with a wry grin, just a spark of hope in his eyes, as we part company.

I wander back onto Clarendon Street, with a newfound respect for South Melbourne, the Swans' real spiritual home. I wish them good health and good luck, knowing that if the Swans snare that elusive Premiership flag it won't just be a victory for Sydney.

Fan Profile

Meredith Burgmann

Meredith Burgmann first ran on to the SCG when she was a blonde-haired university student. It was 1971 and the Wallabies were playing South Africa, it was the height of the apartheid debate and Meredith was one of four protesters who invaded the pitch—actually snaring the football at one stage and then a two-month jail sentence. Now a member of the NSW Legislative Council, Meredith is a long-time Swans member, as well as a keen Balmain Tigers supporter. She was also a prime mover behind the Stop Murdoch Campaign which sprang up in Super League's first year. Meredith also won the NSW Parliament's Aussie Rules tipping contest in 1993 and 1995.

I first came across Aussie Rules because I was married to a Victorian who was an Essendon supporter. When the Swans came up here in 1982, he got all excited and decided we should be members.

I started going to the matches. I thought I was going because it was nice for him and he was very excited about it all. I had always been a dyed in the wool rugby league supporter. I'd been supporting Balmain since 1961 when I was a school kid, quite an intense Balmain supporter and I'd organise the footy parties when we made the grand final. But while I was following Balmain, I kept doing the Swannies' stuff. I knew I'd crossed some line when I separated from my husband but I still found myself going to the matches and taking out a membership each year.

When they went through the Edelsten period it really was quite exciting. I remember going to a meeting where we had to vote. It was at the Hilton or one of those big hotels and we had to vote on whether we should be taken over by a private organisation. Everyone who was a member got a vote. There weren't that many members there.

It was a terrible time because we knew that if we didn't vote for Edelsten the Swans would probably go out of existence. But of course no-one really wanted to be taken over by this terrible doctor and his terrible wife. We voted for it and there was only one against it and that was Gavin Cantlon from the Australian Journalists' Association. He was probably right.

I suppose what I was doing was very very gradually switching what had been my enormous loyalty to the Tigers over to the Swans. I actually enjoyed the years when they did so badly. I read an article recently by a bloke who said he was shocked now the Swans were winning because one of the ways he'd actually identified his personality was as someone who supported a losing football team. I used to tell my child, I'm bringing you up to be a graceful loser because you support Balmain, the Swans and the Left of the Labor Party. I took Paddy to his first game when he was three months old. He has always been a Swans supporter.

For many years there were very, very small crowds—just a few thousand. It was a bit like a Sheffield Shield match. I used to go to them for the absolute peace and quiet and the feeling of calm. And there was an inevitability in those years that we were going to lose but it was just really nice to get out there and see your favourite players, so there wasn't terribly much excitement.

In the last few years, I think one of the confirming matches for me was when I suddenly realised we were a good team and we could do anything. We actually lost, but it was that game when we were ahead against St Kilda. It was the match where Lockett took out Peter Caven. We had played very well. Then the following match, I think, we won in the last quarter. It was the most beautiful quarter—Kickett played brilliantly. I can't even remember who we were playing against but it was a beautiful match. And we won. And it was those two matches together when I thought, we've actually got some good players here. We can make a good team.

In 1993 or 1994, the Swans called a meeting of their prominent supporters. They'd always known I was involved, certainly since I've been a Member of Parliament. There were about twenty other people there and they wanted to talk about how to raise their membership. I can remember [NSW Transport Minister Brian] Langton and I talking to them about tribalism. They thought what supporters wanted was facilities. They thought they wanted a club with alcohol and things like that, whereas we said what they want is an ownership feeling, a badge and a vote. We said a vote was very important, that was about the club belonging to the supporters.

It had been, as you know, in private hands. They were deprivatising at this stage and we were trying to talk about the importance of making it clear that it was now the supporters' club again and not Edelsten's or Mike Willesee's or someone else's. Being a League supporter I understood tribalism totally because League exists on tribalism, which is why Super League is going to be so destructive. AFL exists on tribalism too. Adults never switch their footy teams.

For AFL supporters in Sydney it was slightly different. The Swans start off being their second team, a very favourite second team. Then it becomes a bit equal with their old team and then in the last few years I think it's become their real team.

One of the things I liked about the Swans was that you got to know and identify with other people who went to the AFL matches. There was a group of AFL supporters that you identified with. Certainly within the left of the Labor Party there was an enormous bunch. For some reason the Left of the Labor Party became very identified with the Swannies. There was a big bunch of us, including a number of MPs. So I quite liked that tribal aspect. Your mates went out to the game. This year, I think having a character like Lockett is incredibly important because people who don't know much about the sport can recognise him and talk about 'the Plunger'—as Bob Carr is reputed to have done.

What this year [1996] did was get a whole lot of people watching the game that never would have and discovering it's great fun. So, even if we don't do very well next year we'll still have a much bigger following than we've had before simply because people have go to know the characters and they'll come out and see 'the Plunger'.

I actually think that even if the Super League brawl hadn't happened, that Sydney would still have gone mad over the Swans because it was a real rags to riches story. It was just so phenomenal to have the rise of the Swannies, who were bottom of the heap and everyone laughed at. There were Swans jokes. So to have them go from bottom then twelfth then first was just such a remarkable story.

And they did it with a bunch of characters like Derek Kickett and Lockett and Paul Kelly. They had the hero, they had the comic, they had the bright young boys, they had Plugger. I think what happened would have happened anyway but the Super League stuff was so depressing to the

177

average League supporter that they also moved towards the Swans.

We've got absolutely ambivalent feelings towards the Swannie-come-latelies. On the one hand, we're really glad they're there and that the Swannies are winning matches and have got lots of fans. But at the same time we hate them because instead of arriving five minutes before the game and parking just outside and walking up to your favourite seat, you now have to get there hours early and park miles away and sit in the rain because you can't sit in your favourite seat. It is much more uncomfortable.

My fondest memory of 1996 was the West Coast game because we sat in the pouring rain. It was terrible weather. We sat there and they won and we knew that when they won that match they would be top of the table. It was that wonderful feeling of being there. As long as they won they'd be Minor Premiers. My eighty-one-year-old mum went home after the game and had a heart attack and ended up in hospital on Monday and was still happy.

The worst memory without doubt was the grand final. I drove all the way to Victoria for the game, having stood in the queues and got the tickets for myself and Paddy. But on the way down I got such a bad gastric attack that I couldn't go to the game. I couldn't even watch it on television. I gave my ticket to my ex-father in law, who took Paddy to the match. Then I spent the Sunday driving back to Sydney. Thank goodness they didn't win!

Minor Premiers

The headlined blared out from the front page of the after-noon edition of the *Telegraph*: 'Premier's Plugger Plea'. NSW Premier Bob Carr, known for his love of American history, walking and disdain for all things sporty, was coming out as a Swans fan, penning a reference for Tony Lockett's tribunal hearing. 'The Swans need Tony Lockett. Sydney needs Tony Lockett and the AFL needs Tony Lockett. I don't hesitate to offer my profound support for him,' the Premier's letter read.

It was the perfect fusion for sport and politics; an issue which had engulfed the entire city, drawn inexplicably to this weird new game. Plugger was male lead, the star the script was based around. The previous week the big fella had been reported after being accused of using his elbow against the head of an Essendon player. In his earlier life, Tony Lockett had used these tactics more than once. The most celebrated occurred when Lockett was playing with St Kilda against his new team. A Swans' player called Peter Caven collected a spectacular elbow in the face, smashing his nose. The brutal hit was replayed constantly through the week, the only media the game had received all season, apart from the weekly report of the Swans' lengthening losing streak (this time a one-point loss after carrying a 50-point lead into the final quarter). Caven actually gained minor celebrity status from being on the pointy end of the elbow; earning himself a censure from the AFL for appearing on Andrew Denton's show and thumping a cardboard cut-out of Plugger the thug. But thug no more. Caven was now an Adelaide Crow, while Our Tony was Sydney's golden-haired boy now and never played dirty.

Whether Carr's intervention held any sway, Plugger managed to get cleared by the tribunal. But his bigger problem came from an incident that occurred in the final moments of the Essendon loss. Heading for a three-goal defeat after being well in the match, played at the MCG in front of nearly 70,000 people, Plugger chased a player out to the boundary in one of his traditional intimidatory attacks. In the process he aggravated a groin injury he had been secretly carrying for several weeks. Throughout the week there were questions about Plugger's fitness, but all reference was to a knee injury, part of what was to be a month-long game of foxing by a wily Rodney Eade.

The West Coast Eagles were one of the glamour sides of the 1990s. Entering the competition in 1987, the Wiggles, as they were affectionately known, became the first non-Victorian side to win the comp in 1992, followed it up with another flag in 1994 and had finished a credible fifth the previous year. This season they were in the top four, along with Sydney, Brisbane and North Melbourne. The final order would be dictated by the final round, although there was consensus that West Coast would be there at the business end. The Wiggles were an awesome side at the WACA, a huge dry, hard arena to which their fast and expansive attacking game had been tailored. Their game had translated across the Nullarbor, where they lifted themselves at semi-final time on the big MCG. But the Sydney Cricket Ground was a totally different proposition. For one it was much smaller. More importantly, it had been hit with heavy rain for forty-eight unrelenting hours, leaving huge puddles on the surface—and one-quarter of the sell-out crowd opting for a warm night at home in front of the live telecast. More surprising was the fact that 30,000 Sydneysiders decided to front—including Bob Carr, Eddie, Juzzo and me.

As rain pelted down, we rugged up and threw our shoulders to the elements, ploughing across Moore Park three hours before kick-off in the hope of getting a seat under cover. Not only did we score the seat, but we got the second half of the warm-up game. The match was between the Sydney–ACT Rams and Prahran under-19 sides. These kids were playing for a spot in the draft, but in the wet they looked like drunken lunatics trying to weave through a crowded bar. Wet weather football was a totally new game for me—all fumble, rumble and tumble. The ball is chased from one end of the field to the other, barely a goal scored to upset the, er, flow. It was looking like being a long, cold, wet night. For the first time I conceded the benefits of beanie and scarf outweighed their aesthetic recoil.

As kick-off approached, the rain eased up, although thankfully, not before it had shortened the boot-scooting exhibition. After a season of home games we'd had it all: sheep-dog trials, second-rate pop acts, Korean fireworks. Why the organisers actively encouraged these extravaganzas, while steadfastly refusing to let the kids out on the ground to have a kick remains the season's greatest mystery.

The Swans, sans Plugger, enter the arena to a soggy, but spirited crowd. A strange-looking bloke in a Beanie tosses the coin and Sydney is running with the galeforce wind; although it swirls around the grandstands unpredictably.

The first thing you notice is the step up in class. Compared to the under-19s who had spent the bulk of the match with their butts in the air, the seniors are surehanded and precise.

Not to say it's your dry-weather running game, but the skills that thrill in the dry also shine through in the mud. Guys like Derek Kickett, who always seems to have the ball on a string; Paul Kelly, who runs through anything if the ball's on the other side; and Andrew Dunkley, with his terrific pair of defensive hands, are in their element, winning the 50–50 possessions with a messy type of grace.

I've seen many games of League in the wet at North Sydney Oval. The script would normally go like this. Both sides hit the ball up for five tackles then kick for position for the first forty minutes. No mistakes with the ball. Maybe a try from a dummy-half charge or a spilt bomb. Then they do the same in the second half. Then Norths lose. In contrast, a game of Rules in the wet has the bash and barge, but it also has the high flying marks and desperate snaps for goal. Now it has soccer as well: Dale Lewis dribbling the ball towards the post, before centring it to Stuart Maxfield who strikes clinically for the first goal of the match.

The wind is also coming into play, the ball floating down-field off Sydney boots, while it keeps dropping short for the Wiggles. When Troy Luff bursts onto a Maxfield intercept, we see how strong the advantage is, the heavy ball easily travelling 48 metres to goal. Wade Chapman, a star in the early rounds, is committing himself to every contest, one of those rare breed (that includes Paul Kelly) who seems to have that extra desire to get to the ball first. Just back from a broken foot, he runs headfirst into a West Coast knee and back onto the injured list.

Greg Stafford snaps a point. The big ruckman is right in the game with lots of breakdowns in play forcing ball-ups and throw-ins. Around the ruck he taps and clears, running between zones to secure loose kicks. It's scrappy play, but there's art to it as well. The ball criss-crosses the 50 metre line, no-one in control, but desperate hands constantly propel it in new directions. Brad Seymour, who is playing

182

further upfield than usual, taps the ball through to Kickett; a seemingly random touch finds Kelly, in support, as always. He snaps, but instead of the ball arcing elegantly towards the posts, it runs at a 45 degree angle—along the ground. Luff races after the ball and wrestles with a Wiggle defender for possession. The Swans' unsung hero finds Craig O'Brien, who doesn't miss shots from 30 metres, no matter what the weather.

It's 21–2 and Sydney is settling into the play, finding the loose players and improving its position relentlessly. Upfield through Kickett, Dyson, Cresswell and Stafford, each in a slightly better position across the centre of the ground. The big ruckman winds up and hits a goal from 45 metres. West Coast finally gets around Andrew Dunkley when Peter Sumich snaps a wobbly goal from 25 metres. But when Daryn Cresswell shoots blind from outside the 50 metres, past the West Coast full-back to bounce through the posts, Sydney is up by 27 points at quarter time.

The roles are reversed in the second term. With the breeze it's West Coast who look dangerous, Sydney who is trying to scramble its way out of trouble. It's a different challenge for the Swans; not just getting to the ball first (which players like Kelly do instinctively), but then progressing it downfield quickly enough to mount a meaningful attack with freezing wind and stinging rain howling into your face. At the same time, knowing that if the other team gets the ball, all they need to do is lay it on their boot and it will fly. Sumich snaps his second, then Mitchell White scores through a vacant Sydney square from at least 70 metres out. Either that was a freak kick or the wind is galeforce. When West Coast hits again, this time from 75 metres, we know what the answer is.

Sydney legs are starting to wobble. West Coast mounts a series of assaults, only its crooked kicking keeping the Wiggles in arrears of the Swans. In the final four minutes they spray through four behinds, most the result of ambitious attempts to match the two reefing half-fielders, but also the product of a Trojan defensive effort from Dunkley, McPherson, Seymour and Hueskes.

At half-time I line up at the bar and see a bemused Premier, at his first footy game, up on the TV screen matching wits with Garry Wilkinson. It's not easy, I think to myself. One minute you're writing Plugger a reference, the next minute they have you up there as some sort of football expert being asked questions about the wind on a night when half of Sydney looks like being de-roofed. All in a day's work, I suppose.

Like all good politicians, Bob Carr had gravitated towards the magic. It was like Olympic tickertape parades and Hawkie and Farnsie arm in arm on Australia Day. Cynics see only the snatch for reflective glory; but it's also an official recognition of the Swans phenomenon. Like saying this is something that means so much to so many people that leaders will ignore it at their peril.

In publicly aligning himself to the Swans, Carr was joining a long tradition of patronage of AFL sides by politicians. They were often genuine bonds, built on passion for the game, but not in total ignorance of the mutual benefits. Like John Elliott and Carlton, where the club president could use club functions as a public forum on the NCA. Or Bill Kelty, whose passion for the Bombers threatened attempts to demonise him by the mainstream media. Even Paul Keating gave it a try, making Collingwood part of his vision.

My theory is that politics and footy, especially Rules, are closer than we think. They offer many converging themes. I'm not talking here of the politics of doctrine and ideology, the International Socialists and right-wing think-tanks, but the reality of modern politics; the responsibility of running social policy and an economy in the centre of a torrent of competing internal and external pressures. At the end of the day, politics and footy are both about handling chaos, controlling the vagaries of the bouncing ball while never losing sight of the wider perspective. Running the ball away from goals in a bid to set up an attack, punching for the line rather than risking conceding the mark, always looking for the unmarked team-mate.

Both are about finesse: managing and harnessing chaos because it's inevitable rather than trying to avoid it. There is one significant difference of course; one has a direct influence on the population's quality of life while the other is just a game. I'm just not sure which is which.

The field gets heavier as the game progresses. The second half begins to more mad rumbling through the mud. Here's how play goes: soccer, scramble, stumble, snap. And back again, players throwing themselves from all directions, up and down the field with the intensity only elite sportsmen can muster. Sydney begins to show how much it is missing Lockett. Without the obvious focus of attack, the Swans are forced to probe for an opening around the top of the attacking circle. Stafford shoots high and wide. Kickett snaps crookedly. The Swans are pressing but, like West Coast at the end of the second quarter, failing to convert.

Then Mark Bayes is called off the bench to showcase his poise and experience, seizing control of a bouncing ball and feeding it to O'Loughlin, the smoothest of all the Swans. O'Loughlin dummies, steps into space and kicks truly from 20 metres out. Straight from the restart, it's Bayes again, storming around the boundary line after Kelly and Hueskes combine to clear the ruck. Bayes intercepts the Hueskes roost just inside the boundary and swings the ball centrefield to Grant. After appearing to be fouled around the neck, the boy genius grabs the loose ball and passes calmly to Garlick, who takes the lead out to 19 points with an assured drive from 35.

West Coast replies with a snap after McPherson is isolated in defence, perhaps the first real error of the night by the

Swans back men. Then it's the Wiggles defence looking silly, conceding a rare free kick for holding the ball when a defender dives in to control a bouncing ball. Garlick gets the simple shot from close range to keep the margin at 19 points. But unlike Sydney, West Coast is managing to kick a few goals into the wind and, when one of their big forwards grabs a mark in front of the posts up the other end, we begin to wonder whether the Swans are making the most of their wind advantage.

As the quarter slips away, Kelly works the ball out of defence with one of his signature bursts through the ruck, before reefing it into the attacking zone. Dale Lewis makes the decisive play, launching himself into a bone-crunching shepherd that clears the path for Bayes to grab the ball and chip it into the pocket at an unmarked Derek Kickett. With all the time in the world, Derek positions himself for the simple mark. The ball spews loose, but Kickett still has time to right himself, regather and drill it home from point blank range. The score takes Sydney's lead out to three goals—not enough if you follow the first half.

The crowd is cold, wet and nervy; as weary as the players. The 'SYDN-EE' chant is a mournful, drawn-out one, like a Wembley soccer crowd warming themselves from the inside with their call as the Swans steel themselves for the final quarter assault.

As predicted, West Coast peppers the Sydney defence for the first ten minutes. Sydney counters by stacking the defensive zone with players and frustrating the West Coast attack with totally committed contests. With Roos, Maxfield and Chapman all injured, Sydney has no interchange bench left and when Rodney Eade wants to send a message, Maxfield is forced to limp onto the wing while Grant takes the phone-call on the boundary line.

After confining the Wiggles to three behinds the tide begins to turn and Sydney starts making headway into the wind and rain—which is, if possible, even heavier. We struggle to make out the action in front of the scoreboard as first Bayes, then Lewis, look set to score only to be reined in by the defence. Kickett misses a snap and Simon Arnott, off the bench after being called up to replace Lockett, soccers in a behind. There is the sense that the Eagles need to make their move soon, still trailing by 16 points with eight minutes to go.

Then West Coast concedes possession after finding touch from a restart. Daryn Cresswell, who has been in the thick of the action all night, works the ball through the centre, finding Grant who handballs through some heavy defence to Derek Kickett. The aging magician is again in space and needs only to turn and snap over his shoulder to score the decisive goal. The crowd rises from soggy seats, fascinated by the arm wrestle, which is now bending our way.

They energise the Swans into another assault; Bayes in the action again, setting up Arnott for a shot from the edge of the 50 metres. Revelling in the big time, Arnott gallops off and threads the ball through from 30 metres. The Swans are up by 29 points with just minutes to go. The scoreboard flashes 'Minor Premiers', and the roar engulfs the SCG. From twelfth to first in twelve months. The old-timers can't believe it. But for us Swannie-come-latelies, it's just the next chapter in the fairytale.

Fittingly, it's Derek Kickett; the player who captivated Sydney all year with his shots at greatness, his sense of showbiz, his preparedness to go for the magic play rather than playing the percentages, who finishes West Coast off. One on one in the forward pocket, he latches onto a Shannon Grant lead and shrugs off his marker with a quick step and a sure snap.

As the hooter sounds, the skies open even further, bucketing freezing rain on the thousands of revellers who defy the security guards and rush onto the paddock to honour the Minor Premiers.

Fourth
Quarter

A Semi in Sydney

And so the Swans make history, their position on top of the table securing their first semi-final in Sydney. The Swans' success was part of a remarkable centenary year for the AFL, which saw three of the four finals played outside Melbourne. An enlightened draft policy and shrewd expansion plan meant that there were now strong outposts right across the country. The full houses at the Gabba, WACA, SCG and MCG were an administrator's dream.

The complex finals series would narrow the top eight down to just two sides over the next month. First up, the top four would play the bottom four sides in the eight: first versus eighth, second versus seventh and so on. This meant Sydney's opponents would be Hawthorn, the glamour team of the early '90s, now in the midst of a heated internal debate over a proposed merger with Melbourne. If they won, the Swans would get a week off before playing for a place in the grand final. If they lost they would get a second chance, moving into a sudden death knockout game the following week.

In the lead-up to the first semi, Sydney had been obsessed by one thing: Plugger's groin. The injury the big man sustained while chasing an Essendon defender at the MCG a month earlier had become front-page news, the city sweating on daily updates of its progress. The official line out of the Swans' camp was that Plugger was a 50–50 chance of playing and Sydney breathed a collective sigh of relief when he was listed in the run-on side. Little did we know that he had pulled out of the side early in the week, unable to break into a jog, and that coach Rodney Eade had been playing one of the oldest games in the coaches' repertoire: the fox. Eade talked up Lockett's chances of playing so that the Hawks would waste their time preparing a defensive plan to neutralise Sydney's main attacking weapon.

It had been a remarkable year for Eade too, a first time coach in the top grade. After being signed on the advice of outgoing coach Ron Barassi, the former Hawthorn and Brisbane player had moulded the Swans into a formidable combination. Eade's strength was harnessing the Swans' scrambling style, personified in captain Paul Kelly, with the tactical smarts to maximise the value of their champion full-forward. He had also shown a knack in utilising the available talent, with players regarded as solid rather than brilliant, consistently shining. When the Troy Luffs and Brad Seymours played above themselves week in week out, the coach deserved at least some of the credit. He also brought some imaginative tactics to the game, including 'the huddle'. The huddle was rarely highlighted on TV, but was a regular feature of the Swans' defensive game. When clearing the ball after conceding a behind, about a dozen players would mill at the top of the defensive 50 before dispersing, the ball finding whichever player had shrugged off his defender.

The tactic underlined the importance of coaches. While it appears a random conglomeration of one on one contests, a game of Rules is heavily dependent on the coach. He dictates the match-ups, the patterns in attack and defence, the positioning of loose players. Perched high in a grandstand, he would relay his instructions by phone via the runners and the reserves, who would sometimes be summonsed to the boundary line specifically to take a message. If Rules was grand theatre, the players the actors, then the coach was surely the director, who stakes his reputation on the quality of the performance. In the week leading up to the semi, Eade had been named all-Australian coach, effectively coach of the year. Roos, Lockett and Kelly had also been selected in the elite squad, Kelly as captain.

The all-Australians were an annual affair to compensate for the lack of international fixtures. Apart from an ill-fated attempt to generate international games against the Irish Gaelic football teams in the late 1980s, national representation had never been a going concern. The Irish games were played at a time the AFL sides were looking to Ireland as a potential recruiting base. While it yielded Jimmy Stynes, the Irish-born 1991 Brownlow Medallist, the strategy never really worked. Neither did the games. They were played under composite rules: a Gealic ball, Gaelic net under a crossbar, but with Aussie Rules behinds. The rules also allowed a more vigorous type of tackling than was normal in the AFL. The result was a combination of confusion and extreme violence, the games typically ending in shambolic all-in brawls. Not surprisingly, the concept was soon abandoned.

As the fireworks erupted around the SCG, the ground packed, save the under-utilised members' area, we discovered that Lockett wouldn't be playing. There is a concerned hush around the ground as we digest this revelation. No Plugger. We would soon find out whether all those Southern detractors were right and we really were a one-man side. The lack of the star full-forward represented a major tactical challenge for Eade. His absence against West Coast had been largely nullified by the atrocious conditions which turned the game into a manic scramble. But on a perfect, still Sydney night, the performance inside the 50 metre circles would surely decide the game. Eade's approach is to mix the make-up in the forward pocket, playing O'Brien up front and partnering him with Bayes, Kickett and Lewis at various stages of the first quarter, moving them up and down the field in an effort to disorient the Hawks defensive line.

From the opening minutes we sense how tough this game will be. The experienced Hawthorn players like star full-forward Jason Dunstall (the second player, after Lockett, to kick 100 goals this year), John 'The Rat' Platten (the fuzzy-haired rover), ruckman Paul Salmon and Chris Langford (who commutes from his home in Sydney to play and train for the Hawks each week) begin assuredly. Inside three minutes the Hawks are bombing high into attack. Roos and Dunkley both go up, but the ball flies free to Dunstall who sneaks the ball goalwards. The crowd is silent as the umpire slowly winds up the arms and signals the first goal of the evening. Thousands of Hawthorn fans who have made the pilgrimage to Sydney roar, while the rest of us look on grimly.

Without Lockett, Sydney is playing a long-range attacking game, moving the ball through the centre of the ground as per usual, but searching for the marks on the edge of the 50 metre circle rather than closer to home. Craig O'Brien, whose nonchalant kicking style belies the length and accuracy of his boot, steps out of the shadow of Lockett. The former St Kilda player who came to Sydney at Plugger's urging, snares possession just outside the 50 and kicks his first goal with a long, reefing kick.

The game is being played with a heightened intensity, players throwing themselves at the ball from all directions. This extra effort contributes to a high error rate with countless kicks missing their mark, forcing rabid chases for the loose ball. The lack of executions, however, doesn't

undermine the spectacle as the teams struggle to break the
seven-all deadlock midway through the quarter. Dale Lewis
and Andrew Dunkley are heavily involved across the half-
back line as Hawthorn pushes the ball forward, Platten constantly threatening down the centre. We groan as the hippie
finds his mark and Shane Crawford kicks Hawthorn's
second goal. But Sydney replies almost immediately when
Lewis, now up the other end, grabs a bouncing ball in the
goal square and somehow manages to kick it around his
body for a close range goal.

Then another defender, Adam Hueskes, moves down
into the attacking line. Stafford wins his first ruck over
the veteran Salmon, punching the ball with feeling. The
ball bounces well for Cresswell who gallops into the clear,
finding Maxfield, who was a surprise choice on the bench.
Maxfield scoops the ball up and passes to an unmarked
Hueskes who drills it through from 40 metres. Sydney has
hit the lead for the first time three minutes before the
break.

Already the dynamics of the match are becoming obvious.
Hawthorn looks far better with the ball. Drilled and deter-
mined, they sweep downfield with a minimum of fuss. In
contrast, Sydney is scrambling, using the home crowd for
added intensity to push them to the loose ball first, ensuring
they win the bulk of 50–50 possessions. It's not pretty football but it has worked all year, and as they go to the break
with a seven-point lead, 40,000 Sydneysiders aren't com-
plaining about the aesthetics.

Hawthorn wipes out the deficit early in the second term
through two quick goals as it ominously steps up a gear.
The Swans are competing just as hard across the ground,
but appear to lack execution. Eade would later describe this
as Sydney's 'worst game since round two', but there is something compelling about the way they play badly. It's all
body-on-the-line stuff, Troy Luff flinging himself at the

195

side, Dunkley fearlessly punching clear at the back, Kelly throwing himself into his work as usual. Up front, O'Brien continues to beat his defenders, who are still adjusting to the absence of Plugger. When he kicks another sweet goal from 45 metres, Sydney regains the lead.

The game continues to seesaw, Hawthorn gets in front with two more goals; Dunstall setting up Daniel Chick, before Mark Graham kicks his first. Sydney is paying for its mistakes, both attacking and defensive. For every goal the Swans kick, they register two behinds, the sprayed kicks often the result of attempts just outside the kicker's range. They're trying too hard. Through the quarter the Swans kick five behinds in succession, frustrating themselves and the SCG crowd, as normally reliable kickers like Kelly and Dyson join the perennial pointers like Cresswell in steering their shots wide. Up in the stand it's agony, especially surrounded by Hawk fans who suggest the Swans might be choking. When Dunstall misses a free from in front seconds before half-time, we suspect the pressure may be working both ways. At half-time the score is Hawthorn 6.5–41 to Sydney 4.8–32, the Hawks' accuracy giving them a nine-point advantage.

It's one of those sporting cliches that the third quarter is the championship round, but the first hint of the game breaker catches us all by surprise. Chick kicks his second to take Hawthorn out to its biggest margin of the game, but it is an incident in the lead-up to the goal that is of much greater import. As the ball bounces dangerously in the Sydney defensive zone, Dunkley and Dunstall race to clean it up. Just before they reach it, their legs tangle and Dunstall falls awkwardly, snapping his cruciate ligament as he hits the deck. Chick cleans up the dregs and snaps truly, but as he celebrates he turns around to see his captain writhing on the ground in agony. As the stretcher comes out we feel a strange kind of justice has been done. Without their star full-forward, Hawthorn is now on equal terms with us. The rest

196

of the night will be a test of the second-rungers, the scramblers, the triers. With these battlelines defined, our hopes and expectations soar.

The vibe of the game has clearly changed as Sydney works the ball confidently downfield, the sort of short, sharp drills they've performed routinely all year. Seymour secures possession on the defensive line and sends the ball through the hand to Cresswell and onto Roos, who's been dominating the half-back line as usual all evening. Roos kicks long from centrefield and draws us out of our seats to find O'Brien, marking on the edge of the ruck. The chunky full-forward boots another beautiful goal from 49 metres to bring his tally for the night to three goals. Sydney continues to attack but fails, as it has all night, to convert opportunities. Luff hits the post from a free kick inside 50, then Shannon Grant kicks wide. Ultimately it's left to O'Brien to again sheet home the advantage, this time marking strongly over the back of Langford to set up a shot from 25 metres.

The momentum shifts back to Hawthorn, with a close-range goal to Graham and a couple of behinds to take its lead back out to 10. In a close game Sydney knows it doesn't want to fall any further behind. The lift is provided by one of the unsung players for the season, Jason Mooney. Mooney, who spent much of the season on the interchange bench, moves up to the forward line and immediately makes his mark on the game, snapping two goals inside ninety seconds, both the result of rousing marks. First Cresswell sends the ball high into the attacking zone, where Mooney leaps over two Hawk defenders. Almost immediately from the restart, it's Maxfield picking out the tall utility player in nearly the same spot. Neither kick is easy, but Mooney strikes the ball truly. A late goal to the Hawks gives them a three-point lead going into the final break, but it's anyone's game with twenty minutes to go.

The final result in tight games usually comes down to one

or two definite moments. Dunstall's injury had clearly dulled Hawthorn's attack, but the key plays were still to come. It boils down to which side can pull off something special under the extreme pressure of a semi-final. I had read about the two battles every sportsman faces at the elite level; the one against the opponent and the one within, the battle to silence the internal doubts and do the simple things right when they counted. This would be the Swans' ultimate test against themselves.

From the restart Sydney attacks and it's the honest toilers, the cogs who have kept the Sydney machine turning over all season, who show they're able to handle semi-final pressure. Garlick, Cresswell and McPherson combine out of defence to find Simon Arnott. Arnott unleashes a perfectly placed bomb and it's Jason Mooney, again looming large at full-forward, using his hip to shrug off the Hawk marker and diving full-length to set up his third successive kick. Mooney's is the headline contribution, the type that changes a game tangibly. But it was the finesse of his team-mates that had placed him in the position to make a name for himself.

Now it's Sydney by three points and we are shown how mistakes can be just as vital as marks and goals. O'Loughlin marks near the forward line but sends an atrocious centre kick straight to Hawthorn. The ball runs to Platten who hares off in a zigzagging run, trying to get clear of Justin Crawford. The ground roars when the umpire penalises Platten for running too far with the ball, the first free of its kind I've seen all season, but one which, following home side etiquette, I'm convinced is legitimate. Crawford sets himself for goal from 30 metres, but kicks the ball straight into the marker. The glorious incompetence whips the crowd up as the players compensate for their errors by throwing themselves at the ball with even more conviction.

It's no surprise when the toughest trier of them all makes

his mark. Kelly steals the ball on the half-forward line after it clears the pack from a Hawthorn clearance kick and goes sprinting towards goal. He lets fly a mighty roost from 55 metres which hangs in the air interminably. The Hawthorn defenders dive at the ball and punch it away but the goal umpire sends the SCG into a frenzy by ruling the ball has already cleared the goal-line. It's Sydney by nine.

Hawthorn bounces off the canvas with a goal and three behinds to level the scores. The Hawks ominously begin to control the centrefield, while the Swans struggle to maintain their intensity. Twelve minutes from time and the scores are level—the 'Sydney' chant goes up around the ground, more a mournful mantra than a sharp battle cry.

Then a miracle goal renders us senseless. Stuart Maxfield comes tearing down the left flank, letting rip with a wild speculator just before he tumbles over the boundary line and into the fence. The crowd rises as one, as the ball soars directly through the posts from the most acute of angles. 'Those sorts of kicks don't score goals,' we scream, calling for a drug test, a reality test, something to help us get a grip. But Hawthorn forward Tony Woods proves it's a night of magic, replying with an impossible right-footer down the other end.

The tension is mounting as the game edges towards the type of cliff-hanger that wipes out all memory of the mediocrity of the previous three and a half quarters. Straight from the restart Shannon Grant snaps up the centre bounce, under the noses of the Hawthorn tall timber. In one motion he gathers and kicks, finding O'Brien, again on the edge of the circle. Sydney's most valuable player all night calmly kicks his fifth goal, proving once again Sydney is much more than a big bloke with a Mullet.

Playing what is possibly its last game ever, Hawthorn again rallies. An ex-Swan evens the scores when Darren Kappler, who called the SCG home during some of the darkest years, runs into an open goal and drills the ball low at the man in the white jacket.

It's 84-all with three minutes to go. The roar envelopes the ground as the play continues madly. Close games in Aussie Rules are like no other sport. I suspect it's because of the absence of control. In League a good side can kill sixty seconds in a tight game with a regulation set of six and kick for touch. Not in Rules. Every second is a contest, and when it's even scores in the final minutes of a semi-final, every contest is its own epic battle.

The class players put their hands up as the seconds tick down. Dunkley retains his ascendancy on the full-back line clearing a dangerous attack with a well-judged punch. Then he marks strongly centrefield, killing a Hawthorn thrust. He sends a signature wobble out to Maxfield, who finds Roos unmarked. He coolly sends a high missile from outside 50 metres into the goal square. There are at least five players waiting, but one of them, Darryn Cresswell, leaps highest and seems to hang in the air as the ball hits its target. When he returns to terra firma he has the ball in his grasp and an easy kick at goal in his sights, even for a man who has kicked 21 behinds for the season. When he slams it through, Sydney is six points up with fifty seconds to go.

The clock winds down as Sydney kills time, marking across the paddock. The Hawthorn players know it's all over. Hundreds of supporters stream onto the field, again thumbing their noses at the authoritarian announcer warning them that they'll be arrested. Arrest us all, the mass invasion replies. Meanwhile, Hawks fans weep openly as their heroes trudge off. In their pain, I recognise more of the passion of this crazy game. They've come so far, but their story is over—maybe forever.

A Sydneysider in Melbourne

Sid Marris

I heard it a hundred times: 'What do you know about football? You're from Sydney.'

There is a certain venom in the way that some Melburnians say the word 'Sydney'. A mix of hate, jealousy and a touch of superiority all rolled into one. I learnt early on if they wanted to say something positive they would say 'the Swans', but if they were saying something negative about the Bloodstained Angels it was 'Sydney'.

So what about the Sydney Swans in season 1996? It was not the same as the dislike for the West Coast Eagles, the first team to 'steal' a Premiership from footy's homeland. And it was certainly not like the hate for the Adelaide Crows, whom Victorians especially despise.

When it came to the Swans. Melburnians were confused. They always had a soft spot for the old South Melbourne team—at least until we started winning.

At the same time a funny thing was happening. Around Albert Park the old fans started coming out of hibernation. Retired couples in their weather-beaten cottages with neat, trim gardens were hanging out the red and the white for all to see. By grand final week the local pubs were organising parties to watch the game.

A Swans game in Melbourne is different from any other interstate match. With the Crows or the Dockers, a goal or a spectacular mark or a clever piece of play would at best be greeted with polite applause or the lonesome cheer of some expatriate. Not the Swans. The old South Melbourne brigade—and the ring-ins like me—were always there to make some noise.

And the Swans played as well in Melbourne as they did at home. I remember round 15 at Waverley against St Kilda. Cold with intermittent rain, pure Melbourne weather. The Saints probably had two-thirds of the fans but the Swans supporters made it seem almost even. It was a mixed performance by the Swans for most of the match. Except for the third quarter when they blitzed the Saints, just shifting up gears when they needed to, then dropping back once the game was theirs. As I waited for the traffic jam to ease in the mud-soaked car park, I listened to the radio. They were starting to talk about the impossible: the Swans could make it to the top of the ladder or even the Big One.

I came to Melbourne in January 1996 with work. My father had lived down the road from Brunswick Street Oval in North Fitzroy so I had grown up with Aussie Rules. I lived in Canberra and then moved to Sydney, where I played a couple of B division games in the local comp. When you gave information like this to a Melburnian they would look at you disbelievingly. They also didn't believe it when I said I had been going to Swans matches for ten years. OK, that was back when they were winning too, but I did go to some matches during the low times.

Then there was the really tough question: 'Who did you go for before?' If you answered that one you were stuck. 'Real footy fans don't swap clubs!' they would say with relish. I worked with a woman who also lived in Canberra and went for Hawthorn because her grandmother lived there. She later found out the grandmother actually went for Carlton, but she had decided on the Hawks and that was that. Similarly, just because I moved to Sydney one year after the Swans and lived there until 1995 didn't matter. In her eyes I just went to prove what a fickle, fair weather bunch Sydney Swans fans were.

It got worse. During the ill-fated Hawthorn–Melbourne merger, the passion turned to outright anger against the AFL administration and the interstate clubs for stealing the 'Victorian game'. And then as the end of the season approached, it looked like there was only going to be one final in Melbourne. The friendship was really being tested.

But by grand final day Sydney was back in the fold—even if they still had a lot to learn. Players turning up in their standard grey team gear instead of red and white for the annual grand final day parade down Swanston Street drew muttered comments. And there were the angry glares from the diehard North fans in the minutes before the opening bounce. But once the Big One was under way it didn't matter. Sydney had made it and it was good to be a Swans supporter in the home of football.

Bears, Bombers Bomb

It's six o'clock and we're finishing our pre-game drinks at the Bat and Ball. You Am I is blaring from the jukebox, neatly capturing the mood of the evening: manic, with a soulful edge.

In any other year I would have been here at midday, preparing for that rare moment in any Bears fan's life—a semis appearance at the SFS. In past seasons these had been rare delights, a ritual where a willing crew of old-time Bear fans would work themselves into a catatonic state, knowing they had history in their grasp. This year, true to my resolution, I stayed away, contenting myself with the television replay.

I had monitored the Bears' final assault on the Premiership with mixed feelings, tempering my knee-jerk support with the expectation that they would eventually fall over as they had so many times before. But this year they had acquired a strong young back line in the confusion of the Super League shenanigans, giving them a new dimension—pace and flair. Never before had these twin accusations been levelled at the Bears, but now they were scoring tries from all over the field. Even in the heady seasons of 1991 and 1995 they had ground out their successes in dour forward struggles; now the Bears were playing attractive football.

As the League season struggled on through bogus Test matches and half-hearted Origin series, Norths had gained in stature until they were seriously being considered a Premiership threat. A fortnight earlier they had knocked over Brisbane at Lang Park on the back of some sharp backline plays and dogged second half defence. Now it was accepted wisdom that they would defeat St George, who they had thrashed 42–nil earlier in the year, and progress to their first grand final since 1946—ironically, just twelve months after the Swans reached the play-offs. As the Bears' chance of total victory grew, I confronted the very real prospect that my foray into Aussie Rules would cause me the ultimate pain, heartache and embarrassment; that freed from the shackles of my support the Grizzlies would finally roar. I had contemplated this looming dilemma: what would I do if the Bears made the Grand? The way I figured it, I had two options: either return to the fold for grand final day and support the Bears with all the gusto I could muster knowing they would surely lose, or ignore them in their moment of glory knowing they would win. After a lot of soul searching, I must confess that I had decided on the first course of action.

As it transpired, I needn't have worried. Norths put on one of their signature semi-final performances. From the early intercept pass, to the dropped kicks, to the missed tackles around dummy half, Norths decided to put their fans through a special ordeal. If one moment summed up the match it was the high ball the Saints put up early in the second half. After clawing back from an early 7–nil deficit, Norths steadied to be down 13–6 and started to get a sniff. As the ball hangs in the air, Norths winger David Hall (who's been through it all in 1991 and 1995) positions himself underneath. Suddenly, Ben Ikin, the nineteen-year-old centre Norths poached from the bankrupt Gold Coast, comes careering across the field. Eyes off the ball, he lunges at Hall, knocking him out of the way and leaving the on-coming Saints backline a clear run for the line. If incompetence can be poetic, this was it. Norths never recovered and trudged through the last quarter-hour of the game knowing they had again done something special to snare defeat.

Friends who were at the game winced when I asked them what it was like. The loss had been gut-wrenching, soul-destroying and inevitable. Norths hadn't needed Super League to kill them off, they did it all by themselves. As for me, all I could think was: thank God I didn't put myself through it again. I hadn't invested the emotional energy in a go-nowhere relationship; I'd said goodbye to the bum and good riddance.

As we headed across Moore Park to the glowing SCG we took comfort in the omens; the red and whites would prevail today. We filed into the packed ground, another sell-out, the fourth since the Geelong match, taking our seats near the boundary line in front of the Bradman Stand. The sky is awash with fireworks as the Mexican wave spirals drunkenly around the stadium. Even me, a conscientious objector to the wave, get caught up in the atmosphere and I lift my glass to my lips as it hit. The atmosphere resembles the final overs of a tight one-day cricket match: there's the certainty that something special is going to happen. The experts are tipping the Bombers to win on the strength of their emphatic three goal victory over Sydney in the second last round and an easy win over Geelong the previous week. It's said reluctantly as if it's their professional duty to inform you of the death of a loved one: Sydney has done tremendously this year but its season ends tonight.

But when Plugger waddles out through the banner at ten past eight the crowd rises as one, thumbing its collective nose at the established wisdom. For the past month, Plugger's fitness has been monitored around the clock by the entire city. The injury sustained the last time Sydney faced the Bombers has led news bulletins in the lead-up to the last two games. First it was supposedly a knee, then a double groin strain which ailed the Sydney goal machine. In the lead-up to each match, Eade stated that Lockett would play. Each time, the big fella pulled out. Sydney had made it through tight games on both occasions, but tonight was different, as Bob Carr put it two weeks earlier, so unwittingly prophetic : 'Sydney needs Tony Lockett'. Throughout the week Eade continued his assurances that Plugger would play even if only 50 per cent fit, yet the suspicion remained that maybe he'd already played his last game for the year. So there was relief, joy, even euphoria when Lockett took the field; he's so dosed up on pain-killers that there's no feeling below the waist, but he's out there.

'SYD-NEEE, SYD-NEEE' the cheer goes up around the ground as play begins, but it's Essendon that makes the running early. James Hird, he of the neat hair, long sleeves and self-satisfied countenance, leads the attack. Soaring in front of Dunkley and Bayes, he marks on the 50 metre line and lays the ball up for the Bombers' big full-forward Alessio, who boots the first goal of the game. Hird's there again minutes later, snapping a goal from 25 metres after an atrocious call from an umpire denies Dale Lewis a defensive mark. Then, guess who? Hird, bombing from 60 metres, a sweet torpedo right into the goal square to a stretching Justin Blomfield. It's 18–0 and Sydney hasn't put a fluid move together. The crowd loses its voice momentarily as Hird single-handedly goes about unravelling Sydney's grand final dream.

Then a decisive moment: Essendon surges towards 50 metres again, with Hird leading for a mark. He hits the ground with Dunkley close behind and as the ball goes loose, Dunkley sticks with him, a flurry of elbows as the two wrestle on the ground. Hird gets up, blood streaming from his face, and heads to the interchange for some stitches. His absence would disrupt the Bombers' roll; despite a Cockatoo-Collins snap from 60 metres to take them to 25–1, their domination across half-forward is over. When Hird returns from the blood bin, it is Dunkley who is getting in front and taking the marks. Whether it is the blow to the head or the time spent off the ground, Hird has lost his ascendancy. But for Dunkley, there will be a much greater price to pay.

Down the other end, Plugger is trying to work his way into the game after a month on the sidelines. Each time the ball heads Sydney's way he makes his run. But his timing and the delivery from his team-mates are both awry. The Swans' attacks result in points rather than majors. And at 27–1 down five minutes from quarter time, points aren't what Sydney needs. A goal to Lewis, who marks strongly after a gutsy lead-up from Wade Chapman, back from an eternity on the injured list, gives some hope; but when Rodney Eade stamps out to the centre at quarter time, hissing and spitting at Troy Luff and anyone else unfortunate enough to get in his way, he knows—they know—we all know, that the season is slipping away.

Whatever Eade sprays at the Swans at half-time works, with Michael O'Loughlin leading them back out of the blocks. The lithe Aboriginal centreman launches into the second quarter in a frenzy; attacking the ball from the centre bounce, propelling it downfield with four touches during an 80 metre search-and-destroy mission. Lockett shows the needles are still working by slinging an Essendon defender over the boundary line and Captain Kelly is snaring the possessions that eluded him in the first term. First Kelly points, then he goals from 40 metres after Stafford runs over the top of a Bomber defender. When Plugger finally marks in front of the posts, the crowd lets out its first big roar of the night, knowing the 35 metre kick will bring the Swans back to within one goal. We are knocked back into a stunned silence when the big fella is not allowed to kick for goal because of a bleeding nose. He saunters off, while the crowd boos the umpire; Garlick misses from in front.

Now the North Sydney Bears would be cursing their luck at this point, noting the umpire's dud decision as a valid excuse to be used at the post-loss post mortems. Not our Swannies. First Daryn Cresswell, the man we know and love as 'point', grabs a Lewis lead and kicks from a spot near his Hawthorn triumph a fortnight ago. Then Plugger, back on the field, launches himself through three Essendon defenders at a Derek Kickett speculator and bangs the ball home from in front. The crowd rises as the Swans hit the lead for the first time, having scored 29 of the last 31 points.

Now it's the Swans who are getting to the ball first; exerting their superiority across the ground. From the restart, Stafford gets the tap and Kelly runs onto the ball and out of the centre square, chipping at Kickett. The ball goes loose but the Swans pressure forward; Chapman snares the ball and passes to Cresswell who sees Lockett free. The ball drops short of Plugger but he chases it towards goal, soccering it off the ground towards the posts and careering towards the hapless Bomber defender, those extra kilos acquired over the past month now an asset. The defender deflects the ball back into the path of the rampaging Lockett, who runs across the face of goal like a League second-rower, fending Troy Luff out of the way before snapping over his shoulder with his left boot. The entire passage has taken less than forty-five seconds. Plugger is back and Sydney is in control.

It's Sydney by 14 at half-time and we revel in the amazing comeback that has now seen Sydney kick 48 points to two. But, if I've learnt anything this season and from years of heartache with Norths, it's not to celebrate too early. The beauty of Rules is that when a team gets on top, it can dominate play, scoring at an incredible rate. Sometimes it's the bounce of the ball that will change momentum, but more often it's the weight of pressure from one team that breaks their opponent. For the first ten minutes of the third quarter Sydney continues to attack, but desperate Essendon defence confines them to a behind. Despite their best efforts, the Swans are just two goals clear.

Nine minutes before three-quarter time, O'Donnell kicks Essendon's first goal since the nineteen minute mark of the first quarter. Dale Lewis replies with his second, Chapman again the instigator, but the monkey is off the Bombers' back. Three quick sharp goals tip the balance back in their favour: Wallace receives a penalty in front, Hird soars to mark near the sticks then Alessio goals after a Stafford error. The assault has been fast and brutal; Essendon goes to three-quarter time one point up.

Now it's the business end, and that scintillating draw all those months ago, when Sydney's three-game winning run was sure to end, replays in our minds. The atmosphere is marred only by the Paul Kelly video on the big screen telling us to stay off the ground after the game. The players return to play out the final chapter. But it is the Bombers that kick forward; Hird again on the end of a great Cockatoo-Collins run, to go six points up. Both sides scramble, swapping behinds, searching for that lift to get them over the line. Will it be Kelly, still attacking the ball down the flanks? Or Kickett, yet to produce his magic for the match? Then Mark Bayes, Sydney's longest serving player, makes his mark, though not in the manner he planned. His shocking clearance kick lands in O'Donnell's grateful arms and then Symons nonchalantly bends the ball through. The ground is in shock—Essendon by 12 in a 26-point turnaround. Four minutes to go.

Slowly the chant builds, 'SYD-NEE, SYD-NEE, SYD-NEE, SYD-NEE'. The converts are not prepared to give up yet and neither are the eighteen bloodstained angels. This is the moment they've played for all year, spending countless hours on the same piece of turf, running length of the field drills. If ever that dedication was going to reap a return, this is the time. But it's Essendon who surge again from the centre bounce, deep into the Swans' danger zone. As pressure mounts, Adam Hueskes, the young defender who gained instant celebrity status that morning after the *Sydney Morning Herald* published photos of him dressed in a pink netball skirt and black fishnet stockings, bursts onto the loose ball. The new Dennis Rodman fights through two Bombers and gets the ball to Captain Kelly who sees Stuart Maxfield, the flier, unmarked centrefield, just like at training. Maxfield's away; one bounce, two bounces, 40 metres downfield towards the 50. He lets rip with a long torp right into the square, a perfect length, straight into Lewis' hands. The lazy, erratic and occasional genius has taken his third big mark of the game, all while heavily defended. Now he steers home his third goal and Sydney breathes again.

The noise builds as the combatants engage. Three ball-ups centrefield feed the tension. Garlick and Chapman combine midfield to find Maxfield clear; he chips into the 50 metre circle and finds Lockett unmarked. The crowd roars as he gathers the ball; he's 45 metres out, round near the boundary line, but this is Plugger—he can kick it from anywhere. As the Essendon heads drop, Cresswell moves into space closer to the posts and Lockett, maybe because of the groin, does something he would rarely ever contemplate. He lobs the ball infield towards a better positioned player. From 40 metres, Cresswell strikes the ball truly, his 21 behinds now a distant memory, and drives it through the big sticks, raising his arms high the moment it leaves the boot. 69-all, one minute to go.

41,731 fans are on their feet, screaming maniacally, trying to transfer that last ounce of energy which will get their heroes home. This is the symbiotic relationship between spectators and spectacle at its purest, each fan wondering what they can do to make a difference, not passive observers but active participants in the action. Sydney bursts downfield, but Essendon regathers. Play breaks down in the centre square and just seconds remain. Stafford taps, Dunkley, Kelly, O'Loughlin combine but the Bombers regain. Essendon clears and the crowd goes into a frenzy as the ball floats straight to Wade Chapman, who collects it on the run. Taking a handful of steps Chapman bombs the ball into the 50, down to Lockett, who grabs the ball right on the edge of the circle. If we weren't already crazy, we'd be out of our seats. As it is, the hysteria goes into overdrive.

And so the season has come down to this. The perfect script. Plugger from 60 metres, no feeling from his waist down, long-suffering Sydney fans and Swannie-come-latelies all willing him on. The kick would normally be in range, but with his dicky groin, it's his longest attempt of the night. It doesn't even need to be straight, it can just wobble through for a point and we won't mind. The final siren sounds. This is the last kick of the game. Lockett moves in, a barely perceptible stutter in the run; bent low, the giant frame dwarfing the ball as it has done more than a hundred times previously this year. Plugger lets rip and the ball takes off, onwards and upwards to victory.

As the goal umpire signals the point, the ground explodes. Thousands ignore Kelly's tele-request and storm the field, the Swans' song ringing out across the ground. The Swans have formed a giant pile of bodies on top of Plugger on the 50 metre line, while the Bombers leave the arena, dazed and confused. The Swans have completed their transformation from ugly ducklings and are on their way to Melbourne, a

Bears, Bombers Bomb

showdown with the Southerners neither they, nor us, had ever seriously contemplated.

Into the night we go. Sydney is celebrating, the Saturday night pubs around the SCG awash with red and white. Those who haven't seen the game demand a recount. One lad tells me how he was walking down the street near full-time, heard cheering from inside a house and knocked on the door demanding to see the end of the game. We drink and talk about Plugger; his groin, his Mullet, his kick. We sing the Swans' song again as the band in the Hopetoun Hotel takes a break between sets. Everyone in the pub joins in—they all know the lyrics. I turn to my comrades, teary and beery: 'Friends,' I say, 'we're going to Melbourne.'

Luff is in the Air

*Of all the Swans, Troy Luff is the SCG crowd's favourite,
the Dougie Walters-style larrikin who has always captured
the Hill's imagination. The tall blond utility would turn up
on the forward line or down the wing, take the big mark,
kick the vital goal, play as the Swans' bonus star. What
made Luffy all the more popular was that he's a battler, a
player cut (twice) by the Swans when they were at their
lowest point, yet a stand-out performer when they turned
the corner. Luffy personified the Sydney resurgence, a
reminder that perseverance pays off and, when he kicked
two goals in the first quarter of the grand final, proof that
fairytales sometimes (almost) happen.*

Where did you begin your career?

I grew up in Traralgon, about 160 kilometres east of Melbourne, in the La Trobe valley.

An Aussie Rules town?

Big time. Big players like Kelvin Templeton, Geoff Jennings,

Bernie Quinlan played for Traralgon before they went else-where. I was born there and lived there for seventeen years until I moved to Nelson Bay in 1986 with my family.

I also hear your mum used to play.

Yeah. They had a women's league, a couple of games a year and she actually had a knee reconstruction after playing a game of football.

Did you go to the games?

Yeah, I went and watched. It was pretty ferocious stuff, but she was a pretty good player.

Were you a gun player in Traralgon?

All through juniors I was sort of up there each year. I never considered myself a gun but I was one of the better players. I only played one year in Traralgon in the under-18s before I left, anyway. My father got a job in Newcastle and moved north. We had the choice of living anywhere within 100 kilometres of Newcastle, so we moved to Nelson Bay which was a really nice place.

So did you get into the surfing?

No, my brother did, but I just couldn't handle it. I tried surfing, windsurfing, tried all that but I'd rather just go out there and bodysurf.

Any Aussie Rules up there?

Yeah. They won the flag this year; they won the flag two years ago. When I was up there we played in three grand finals and lost them all. The Newcastle competition plays for the oldest sporting trophy still contested—that's the same trophy they were playing for a hundred-odd years ago and it was inducted into the Newcastle museum this year. There's been a few patches, like in the early 1900s, when they stopped competition for a while, but Aussie Rules has been strong in Newcastle for well over a century.

Was your path into the Swans playing well in Newcastle?

They asked me down a couple of years before I actually came. I played a couple of junior games, a few country versus city games, then finally during 1990 they said come and have a game in reserves and see what happens. I came down halfway through the season and for something like twelve games I just travelled back and forth from Nelson Bay, both for training and then to play. I was working up there as a swimming pool builder, I didn't really want to leave that and I didn't really want to move to Sydney either. I didn't move here until the next season; I did pre-season here in 1991 and moved down in February that year.

I understand you've actually been cut twice by the Swans. What was the story behind that?

At the end of '94 I was told I was going to be delisted.

How did they do that?

They get you in a room with about four blokes, the team manager, the general manager and whoever; and they say, 'Sorry, the club's enjoyed you being here and you've been great for the club, BUT—you're no longer required'. Then they decided after about a month or so of me not knowing what was going to happen in the future that they wanted to keep me on the list. Then they actually had too many draft picks for the pre-season draft in '95, so because of that, they had to de-list me again and then re-draft me back. At the end of '95, I wasn't sure of my future but with the new coach, he had a bit of input into who stays and who goes, and he obviously wanted me to stay; it was certainly worthwhile staying.

What do footy players do when they get de-listed?

Well you're just in limbo, you've just got to hope that another club has watched you play and thinks you can play. You've got to wait for the draft to be over before you say to yourself, 'Well, I'm not going to be an AFL player this year'. So you've got to go and think where you're going to play next. I had four clubs in Adelaide from the South Australian Football League ring up; as well as clubs from Canberra, Tassie and Queensland.

Would you have taken up one of the offers?

If it came to it I was considering going to Port Adelaide, they were pretty keen and, with the possibility they might have been in the AFL soon, were pretty attractive. So you never know, I might have been playing for Port Adelaide in 1997 against the Swans.

Were you playing through that long losing streak in 1992–93?

Up and down.

What was it like?

Well even when I first started in 1990 we didn't win a lot of games. In 1991 we started to go downhill and '92, '93,

217

'94 I think we finished on the bottom. It got to the stage where you would just be going out and making sure you played well. You were worried about your own football rather than about the team. I think we got the wrong breed of player that came here for themselves, seeing how much money they could earn before they went somewhere else, instead of worrying how well the Swans were going to do. If we had a close game we'd consider it a good game; if we won a game it was time to throw a party. I think towards the end of '94 we started to look good again, we sort of got more of a team spirit going, whereas we'd seemed to miss that a lot in the early '90s.

What sort of footy were you playing then?

It's hard to say. I don't reckon we had any style at all. The years that Buckenara was coaching we just had no system at all. It was just a case of go out and play and hope for the best. Even in Barassi's first year there was no real organisation, but things have certainly changed with Rocket. He's very systematic with what he does.

Does it make the footy more enjoyable?

Certainly. It all comes down to team spirit. There were too many guys who weren't here for the long haul, they were only going to be around for a year or two and they knew that.

Where do you live these days?

Just over in Centennial Park, basically a block from the SCG.

And is it a pretty tight-knit group of players?

218

That's the thing with the Swans. Because we're all from different places, not many guys here from Sydney, we all knit together really well. In Melbourne you've got your outside friends, so you have different groups, in Sydney we're just one big group.

During that long losing streak, is there a point that stands out as the lowest of the low?

I think when we started coming up against the bottom sides and even they were beating us pretty convincingly, games when you thought, we've got to win these. It got to the stage towards the end of 1993 that guys were just counting down the days to the end of the season; there was a calendar up on the wall and it had six weeks and twenty-four training sessions until we were finished. It seemed the guys didn't care about how they were going or how the team was going, just how long it was until the end of the season.

Do you remember the Melbourne game that finally broke the drought?

I didn't play, I was injured. I did my knee about two or three weeks before that and I had to sit in the stands and watch it. I remember afterwards the guys thought it was like winning the grand final, but I didn't really think they should get too carried away with one win.

What happened the week after?

I can't remember, but they probably lost.

That was just after Barassi came in. Was he the turning point?

No, I really think the turning point was the playing staff.

We got rid of the players who didn't want to be here and brought in players who did, especially Plugger and Roosy. There were also the young guys like Chapman, Seymour, O'Loughlin and Garlick who all came in '93 but are still here and starting to become the backbone of the side.

More personally, you seem to have a bit of a roving commission out on the field.

Yeah, I get a bit of everything, on the wing, on the ruck, up on the forward line, everywhere. Each week you're given a role to play, whether it's to tag somebody or to play the half-forward and be the second option to Plugger, or pick up the crumbs, or roam the whole ground, be the spare man in defence—you get a different role every week.

What do you see as your main attributes as a player?

I think being versatile, being able to play a range of positions. I don't think I've got great skills, but good enough to play first grade. I'm probably a pretty good mark.

What about some of the high points of the year?

Definitely running out to play Geelong with the 44,000 here and 500 next door in the Stadium, as we discovered later. That was certainly the most intense crowd I've played in front of; and the fact that we did so well on that day and beat them by so much, it really gave me a tingle in my stomach. It was just so exciting to run out onto the ground and know that most of the people were there for you. I think it was just as exciting that day as it was against North Melbourne in the grand final. And as the year progressed and more and more people kept coming, it just made it better and better.

Your own form seemed to lift with the crowds. People have told me you weren't half the player you were in 1996 in previous seasons. Were you doing anything different?

I don't think so. It was confidence more than anything else and the coach. The coach had confidence in me and faith in me, which made it much easier. The last two years, not including 1996, I was playing good football but every time I got into the side it was only as a fill-in. Even when I did get seven or eight games in a row in first grade, I might have a couple of not-so-good games and all of a sudden I was out of the side again. So the pressure was always on you every week, I was always worried about what I was going to do on the field and whether it would get me dropped next week, and half the time I was playing off the bench anyway, so there was no chance of settling in to a position. This year was different, I wasn't just counting up the number of games I could play in a row, instead it was a case of go out each week and just do what you have to do.

One thing I've always wondered about elite sport: is it actually enjoyable while you're out there?

It's hard. It's enjoyable when things are going your way. I mean, everyone loves getting a kick and when you don't get a kick it's pretty annoying. But this year, even when we lost, it was still enjoyable to play. It wasn't like you were being thrashed by ten goals or making atrocious mistakes to throw it away.

Looking at the finals' series, the first final was against Hawthorn without Lockett. What did you have to do differently that game?

I think we were pretty confident without Plugger anyway. We'd won the week before without him against West Coast and while that was a completely different night, muddy and wet and Plugger might not have kicked a goal anyhow, we were pretty confident that whoever was on the forward line would kick a few goals. We always thought we were going to win the game; it ended up being a lot closer than what we thought, mainly because Hawthorn had a lot of very experienced players.

What do you remember of the Essendon game?

I realised halfway through the final quarter that if we didn't win, the season was over and we maybe would never get the chance to play in a grand final again. I think a lot of guys felt the same thing and lifted when it was needed. To get back in touch we really thought, this is our shot at a grand final. Then Plugger got that final kick; I walked past him and said, 'All you've got to do is get it over the line and we win the game'. He said, 'Thanks for that', then kicked it.

Would you have pulled it off if there were only 10,000 at the SCG?

I don't know. Once you start playing the game, you forget about who's out there. Sometimes when the ball's up the other end of the ground you can hear the noise, but generally once you start playing it's just an unconscious thing to know the crowd's there. It certainly helps when the crowd's going your way. I think it's often a case of the opposition hearing the crowd cheering for us, rather than the other way around.

And what of the grand final experience. Do you remember it fondly or as a bitter disappointment?

I certainly remember before the game, trying to be as relaxed

222

as possible. I ran out on to the ground probably last so I could get a good look at what was going on. As we ran around and did our warm-up lap we looked, as we had discussed before the game, at the crowd and the balloons going up, all the red and white. Then it got down to the national anthem and we stood there and had another look around and thought, right, that's it, we're ready to go. Once we started kicking the ball to each other we got into footy more and we were there to win a game and not for the spectacle.

It worked for you, two goals in the first quarter...

I just went about it as a normal sort of game; once the ball got bounced that was it. You could hear the roar of the crowd going, and then it was time to go yourself. It was pretty exciting stuff.

When did you get the feeling that things were starting to come undone?

I think when Glen Freeborn kicked a couple of late goals just before half-time. We missed a couple in the second quarter which could have made it a big lead for us. At half-time I still didn't worry about it, but late in the third quarter they were starting to get away. We missed a few opportunities, they kicked a few goals. Once the last quarter got under way and they kicked the first goal I started thinking, that's it.

What was it like travelling back to Sydney the next day?

It was disappointing to lose, but it was such a thrill to be there that it just makes you hungrier to play in another one and win. There was also a sense of relief that a very long season was finally over. Once we got back we probably spent a week on the piss, so we didn't give ourselves much of a chance to think about it except for straight after the game.

And what are your feelings about Sydney's supporters after the 1996 year?

I think they were pretty genuine. In 1986–87, the crowds were sort of brought to watch the game, with the glitz and glamour and thousands of free tickets given away. This time around there were no free tickets and people were desperate to get into games. A lot of people say it's 'in' now to come and watch the Swans play, but it's a product of our success and I think now that we've got the supporters in, we've just got to keep them there by playing good footy. I don't think they expect grand finals every year, but if we give them reasonable success they'll become true Sydney supporters, with their hearts in it, not because it's in fashion.

Queues, Conspiracies and Pollie Waffle

I had planned to rise at 7am Monday morning and pick up a grand final ticket on the way to work. There were supposed to be 7,000 tickets for the Swans 10,000 members and I couldn't imagine them all making the trip South. But at 5.30am I jolted awake, bolt upright in bed, convinced I had to leave home immediately.

I showered, jumped on a city bus and headed for the BlockBuster Music store in Pitt Street Mall, one of the designated ticket outlets. About thirty people were there before me, including half a dozen who had clearly slept the night. I'd always wondered whether people really did this, sleep on the streets to get first tickets to a big event, or whether the TV crews just threw a sleeping bag at the first people in line to make a better news story. But here they were, bleary-eyed desperates, still rugged up on the cold pavement, wishing they were still asleep. The more canny early arrivals had their own folding chairs, but I had to content myself with the *Herald* TV guide to keep the piles from the back door. Setting up my morning papers and a mega-cino I began my three-hour vigil.

They say that in the dying days of communism, eastern Europeans used to queue habitually. See a line and the smart thing to do would be to take a place in it and wait for it to grow. When you had established your position, you'd get someone to mind your spot and go to the front of the line to see if you wanted whatever you were queueing for: bread, radio parts, tickets to the grand final. The eastern Europeans really knew how to have a good time. The beauty of queueing is that the longer you wait, the more people are behind you—suckers that you know will need to wait longer. Thus, as the morning wore on and the queue behind me grew, I began to feel better: alive, awake and smarter than everyone to my rear.

The other thing about getting tickets to a big game is that you need to co-operate with fellow humans—even your family. Next to me an uplifting display of filial co-operation is played out. When I arrive a schoolboy, probably fourteen years old, is cooling his heels, killing time with a GameBoy. At about 7.30am a well-dressed man in his mid-forties shows up, gives the kid some lunch money and sends him off to school. We share a coffee and start talking. The boy is his son and has snared the spot in the queue for his grandfather. Dad is just the intermediary, holding the position in trust. Sure enough, at 8.45, the grandfather turns up with his wife and Dad heads off to the office. The grandfather is Bob Reynolds, a Swans fan since he went to school at South Melbourne. He was there at the last grand final, the 1945 'bloodbath' against Carlton. I'm transfixed as he recounts that game, the minutes collapsing in as I learn of the exploits of Clegg, Whitfield and the Montague gang.

Then the doors are now open and we file in for tickets; within twenty minutes I have mine in hand and strut past the hundreds of worried-looking supporters hoping to beat the sell-out. I was one of the lucky ones, hundreds of fans who had risen at 7am to pick up tickets on the way to work would be left clutching at thin air after an under-allocation of seats for Sydney.

Saturday night's victory dominates the Sydney press, totally overshadowing the upcoming League grand final, which everyone knows Manly will win. The match reports focus on Plugger's last-minute kick and the Swans' awesome comeback, but there's a line in the body of the text which takes some of the gloss off the win—Andrew Dunkley was being investigated for the first-quarter scuffle which forced James Hird to the blood-bin. What starts as just a line in Monday's paper snowballs through the week.

In many respects, the Dunkley saga was the classic sports scandal story, the type that keeps journalists occupied between the matches, providing a lever for more pre-game hype. The best scandals even provide a sub-text for the main event, galvanising the themes that run below the surface. Like Phar Lap and the US conspiracy, Dean Cappabianco and the positive drug tests, the murder of the Colombian goalkeeper after the 1991 World Cup. The sports scandal story can, when executed properly, overshadow the actual event.

The Andrew Dunkley story thrived because it provided a solid rock for the North–South rivalry that underpinned the grand final. While Dunkley had not been reported by the umpires, the AFL instigated an investigation on the strength of video footage. On Tuesday the 'investigators' (two AFL employees, although the term conjured up images of Elliott Ness) studied the video, with every indication that the charges would not proceed. While the video suggested a couple of shots may have connected, the angles were inconclusive and the Jerry Seinfeld lookalike looked like he'd walk.

Then the Murdoch tabloids took control. First, Melbourne's *Herald-Sun* got hold of some different camera angles.

Sniffing a cross-Murray war of parochialism, the paper plastered the blurred shots across its afternoon edition and demanded charges be laid. Pressured to action, the AFL then summoned Dunkley to appear before the tribunal on the Wednesday night. 'Low Blow', Sydney's *Daily Telegraph* responded on its front page, suggesting a Melbourne conspiracy against the Swans.

The story thrived for forty-eight hours as court injunctions were sought, the AFL was accused of incompetence and Sydney started thinking about tactics without its star defender. Finally on Thursday, the Supreme Court granted Dunkley an injunction until after the grand final, finding the AFL's four-day investigation had left the Swans insufficient time to mount a defence. 'AFL Red Faces' the *Telegraph* trumpeted. Dunkley was free to play, but the immense pressure would tell on Saturday. He would end up another casualty of the blatherings, death by headline.

As Dunkley dominated the headlines, the Swans became the unlikely focus of state politics. Premier Carr set the tone at the West Coast game, but he was one of many politicians, of all persuasions, who were backing the Swans with bluster and bellicose. If the anti-sporting Premier could jump on the bandwagon, those MPs who actually followed the game felt more than entitled to follow suit.

In the NSW Upper House, MLCs Meredith Burgmann and Jenny Gardiner led the House in a rendition of the Swans' song during the Wednesday adjournment debate. Speaker Max Willis accepted the diversion with bemused acquiescence, as the backbenchers belted the theme out.

But it was in the Lower House that the following urgency motion was debated on 25 September, a line of statesmen and stateswomen placing on the record their long, if sometimes tenuous, associations with the Southern game.

Following are edited extracts from the *Hansard*.

'That this House:

(1) congratulates the outstanding achievements of the Sydney football club in 1996;

(2) recognises the excellence of captain Paul Kelly, Tony Lockett, Paul Roos and coach Rodney Eade in gaining individual all-Australian selection; and

(3) wishes the Sydney Football Club every success in the centenary grand final on Saturday, 28 September 1996.'

Brian Langton (Kogarah, ALP): The success that the Sydney Swans enjoyed this year has had State-wide benefits. The increase in the number of people who have come to Sydney both from rural and regional New South Wales, as well as from interstate to see the Swans this year has contributed enormously to tourism ... I feel particularly proud about next Saturday. I have been playing Australian Rules football since I was about eight or nine years old. In fact, my first visit to Melbourne was as a nine year old with an Australian Rules team. I was fortunate enough to proceed onto the seniors and play Australian rules for St George—though not much of it in first grade.

Chris Downy (Sutherland, Lib): My first experience of a live Aussie Rules game was in 1990 when I saw Geelong play Essendon at Glen Waverley before a crowd of about 98,000. The game was a revelation ... the Australian Rules game is typical of the way sport is heading in this country. Regardless of the code, sport has a truly national focus. Whether it is Aussie Rules, rugby union, rugby league or soccer, Australia has a national focus on sport. It is important to have that national focus and move away from regional and city allegiances. The Australian Football League should be congratulated on a job well done ... certainly the Opposition joins the Government in wishing the Sydney Swans every success in the AFL grand final at the Melbourne Cricket Ground this Saturday.

Maurice Iemma (Hurstville, ALP): It is unfortunate that the mouth from the South, the loud-mouthed Premier of Victoria re-opened the old wounds about the club being just a Melbourne transplant. Indeed, in the early years that was exactly what the team was ... [today], they are far from it. They have won the hearts of the Sydney sporting fraternity. They have expanded into schools. They have done a lot to develop junior Australian Rules football talent in the Sydney competition. That will form the basis for the Swans getting a lot of Sydney-based players in the years to come when many of the senior players retire.

Barry O'Farrell (Northcott, Libs): I am pleased to participate in the debate, in which honourable members have set out their football credentials. Having been Catholic educated, I played both rugby and Aussie Rules at school. With someone of my size it was not too long before they worked out that gravity meant that I could not be a ruckman; I ended playing in the forward position ... at university. I did not have the groin problems that Tony Lockett had. I think it is no coincidence that Tony Lockett's groin miraculously recovered the week the Dalai Lama visited Sydney, and for that I am truly thankful.

Gabrielle Harrison (Parramatta, ALP, Minister for Sport): I feel somewhat disadvantaged in that I cannot stand here and laud my past football exploits. I have tried most sports but unfortunately I have not tried football. I am delighted to support the bipartisan motion relating to the Sydney Swans ... It is often said that Sydney loves a winner and Melbourne loves sport. That is not entirely fair or true. Sydney is full of people like me who have supported Sydney on and off for more than a decade and who are now enjoying the fact that the Sydney football team has finally reached its full potential.

Democracy in action. But for once, the pollies reflected the public's opinion. Across the city it was Swans-mania or 'white-line fever' as a colleague who supported Carlton had described the pre-game nerves on the eve of the 1995 grand final. Media saturation, shops with red and white bunting (and not for St George), organising grand final barbecues, scrambling for a ticket to the big game, trying any contact no matter how tenuous, the city was possessed. It was like Christmas, your birthday and a federal election all rolled into one.

Fan Profile

Bob Reynolds

I met Bob Reynolds and his wife Pat as I queued for grand final tickets. Bob was a special Swans fan—he'd been through a grand final before. It was 1945, the game they call the 'Bloodbath'.

The thing I vividly remember about the game was the brawl. Up 'til the brawl the Swans were in it.

It occurred just before half-time. Incidents started to flare up all around the ground, all sorts of little individual fights and next thing it was all in. The first one to fall, to my memory, was a chap called Ron 'Smoky' Clegg. He was seriously injured with stop marks all the way up his back from the boot or boots of Carlton captain Bob Chitty. That was the incident that was heavily highlighted in the press on the Monday after the grand final.

Clegg was a very good player, a Brownlow Medal winner actually. Once he was interfered with, I think it was a case of everyone trying to rectify the wrong, so called. It went on from there.

The incident certainly upset the pattern of the game and the Swans or South Melbourne as they were then, lost the fight. They were beaten in the fighting and they were beaten in the football.

It was real fisticuffs. Teddy Whitfield of the Swans, in particular, got into the fight as well, like a mad bull covering a lot of the paddock to hit anybody he could get his hands on. After the grand final he was suspended for a year.

The Swans did have some good physical people because South Melbourne is on the border with a place called Port Melbourne where they played football very, very, very tough. It was Association football down there and it was even tougher than the VFL.

There were whispers before the game that it was going to be a very tough match. Carlton had played Collingwood the week before and my cousin, who was a staunch supporter of Collingwood, warned me that Carlton were extremely physical. 'They'll probably physically try to knock you over,' he said. 'No,' I said, 'we'll be able to handle it.' Or so I thought. It didn't turn out that way.

The atmosphere was fantastic. It was played at Princes Park which was the home ground of Carlton. This was because of the war. In 1945 the big grounds like the Melbourne Cricket Ground and the South Melbourne ground had been taken over for the services to be used as camps. Therefore the VFL was forced to go elsewhere.

The game was nowhere near as fast as it is now. It was dominated by high marking; there wasn't so much punching the ball away as most of the opponents were content to out-mark each other. It's only in latter years that they've perfected the punch, just as the ball's about to reach the hands of the chap in front. It was a lovely spectacle back then, even if it wasn't as effective.

The 1945 grand final was well worth seeing, although I was bitterly disappointed when the Swans got beaten. I thought

they had a really good chance but Carlton were far too physical all over the ground. They were a good team and they just
outplayed the Swans, particularly after the fight. The Swans
centremen, in particular, got the stuffing knocked out of them.

Following the match the fight continued. There was a
gang of ruffians who used to inhabit a place called
Montague, which is on the border between South Melbourne and Port Melbourne. They were known as the 'Mont
Gang' and were headed by a chap by the name of Stanley
Bullpitt. A supporter of Carlton crossed the ground after the
match; extremely well dressed, coming across to the stand
section of the Carlton crowd. The Monts turned on him, but
they'd miscalculated. The Carlton fan turned and fought the
whole gang, one at a time. They came up to him and he'd
knock each one down. No-one ever knew who he was, but
he summed up the day!

Since that day there's been bad feeling between Carlton
and the Swans. There'd been no more beforehand than with
any other club but afterwards, every match since then, South
Melbourne or Sydney have often been able to rise to the
occasion. I would imagine that the coaches would push that
'remember 1945' to those that could possibly remember,
and go on from there.

I can recall when we first moved to Wollongong there was
no TV, and I used to go up the Macquarie Pass with my car
and listen to the Melbourne football broadcast. When the
South Melbourne and Carlton matches were broadcast on
the ABC, you'd want them to win that little bit extra.

I grew up in South Melbourne, which was an industrial
suburb at the time. It is more affluent now but back then
there were a lot of gangs around, a lot of hoods. It was a
very, very poor area, one of the poorest in Melbourne. South
Melbourne was famous for the Hoadley's chocolate factory
which stood in Grant Street, now completely taken over by
the Westgate Bridge freeway.

I had aspirations of being in the Navy—it wasn't a suburb of doctors and lawyers. I started following the Swans because my uncle was a member and he used to take me to all of the home matches. I probably would have seen the Swans first in the early '30s.

My first idols were Herbie Matthews in the centre, Ronnie Clegg and before that Jack Graham. He was famous for his place kicking for goal, he would kick for goal straight on, like a League player.

We lived very close to the ground—no more than quarter of a mile away. I would go to my uncle's and away we'd go to the Lake Oval. We would stand, as seats were at a premium—there used to be a row just around the edge of the ground and you'd have to get there real early to get one of them. Everyone else had to stand. There were also seats in the grandstand—a tiny South Melbourne stand but they were for the Trust members.

I played just the one game of third grade amateur—and I was hopeless. But everyone played in the streets; they would kick a paper because they were so poor—they didn't see a real football. You'd play on the bitumen with your newspaper football, wound up tight and tied with string. It was just kicking—no goalposts.

They did play at school but I wasn't good enough. In Victoria that was bread and butter. Those that were good were nurtured, although there was no serious money in the game at that stage, just pride.

But I used to sell the Football Records, at fourpence each. When I was very young—from the age of seven upwards—I'd go on the morning of the match and get a big pile from the newsagent. When you brought the money back they would give you so much for selling the copies.

I came to Sydney in 1949 and didn't hear much about footy right through to the '70s. Then they started to play exhibition matches, then proper matches up here before the

Swans relocated. I used to go to those exhibition games.

My biggest regret of those years is that I missed seeing one of the best players of all time: Bob Skilton, who played for the Swans through the '50s, '60s and into the '70s. He won three Brownlows and I've always been unhappy that I missed out.

I started going again in 1982 when the Swans moved north. We were some of the earliest members. Their very first match was played against Melbourne, which was then coached by Ron Barassi, and the Swans won. Barry Round was the captain and they had a pretty good side, including Steven Allender and Stevie Wright. They had a good season the first season.

This last season was fantastic. It's incredible, because after the first two matches the thought was 'here we go again'. And then the turnaround occurred against the West Coast Eagles in WA where they lost. They played very well for two and a half quarters. That was when the expectations built up bit by bit.

The Big Day

I wake to greet grand final day with a searing headache. I had turned thirty the night before, partied through the night, and needed more pain-killers than Plugger's groin. I grabbed ninety minutes' sleep before jumping in the 5.30am cab to the airport. Taken together, these were formidable numbers. What should have been a seminal rite of passage, a journey to my new life, was shaping as little more than an ordeal of endurance, a battle with body and mind just to last the game. In the parlance of the code I was 'under-done', 'short of a gallop', 'a little but groggy'.

There were chaotic scenes at Sydney airport; hundreds of fresh-faced Swans supporters, up with the sparrows after early nights queue excitedly. I lurch among the red and white balloons, seeking fresh air amidst the Swannie-come-latelies, diehards and desperates. I wonder to myself how many people have missed great days in history because of the night before.

The plane touches down at Tullamarine and I'm ushered to my South Yarra base, not too far from the Swans' historic home in the gentrified suburbs of Albert and Middle Parks. As we drive past the MCG, thousands of fans with standing room tickets are already filing into the ground. The enormity of the day hits me as I collapse for a ninety-minute power nap.

At midday I set off for the 'G' feeling half-human and ready for whatever highs and lows are to follow. Trickles of fans turn into droves coming from all directions to the massive edifice which is the undoubted home of Australian sport. The site of the first ever cricket Test and the 1956 Olympics, the MCG is where sporting history is made. A massive arena, which fits double the spectators of the SCG, the 'G' is encircled by steep stands that perch over the action. It is said the best stadiums evoke the power of dictatorships—stark, imposing, authoritarian. If this is true, the MCG was right at home in Kennett's Victoria.

Our tickets are at the top of the Great Southern Stand, the massive construction which alone seats 50,000 spectators. Onwards and upwards we climb, altitude sickness a real danger as we grip our seats, three rows from the back. The tight seating adds to the disorientation, requiring beer runs to be executed with the precision of a K2 assault. We are cramped and exposed—but lapping up the sort of view most people do climb mountains for. From the top of the Great Southern Stand the field stretches out like a board game, you can see the lines of attack and the holes down the ground. When a player gets into the clear, you can see the how and why. The other thing about the MCG is that it is round. The SCG is an oval, longer than it is wide. The G is symmetrical, vast acres of space out on the wings making the game all the more expansive.

But the real power of the MCG comes not from its size or scale but the swarming mass of humanity it holds. There's 93,000 other people in this arena, 93,000 people witnessing the same event, reacting to the same stimuli. In an era where people are increasingly isolated and disjointed, the television our only common experience, the community of spirit at a full MCG is something to savour. The power of the crowd, all focused on a small red ball, is rooted in its mass. I was in the largest crowd of my life and I felt at home.

As the clock approached 2.15 the pre-game entertainment begins. Never having been a Tina Turner fan, I'd always tried to ignore the League extravaganzas. But today's ceremony provides two important omens, symbols that I'm sure will preface a Swans victory.

The first occurs at the height of the festivities. From beneath giant inflatable footballs emerge two huge effigies of footballers reaching for a mark, extended to full height by hot air. At one end of the field Sydney's Number Four, Tony Lockett sans Mullet, reaches proudly for the ball. But at the other end, North's Wayne Carey buckles. Desperate roadies attempt to right him as the Swans fans roar their appreciation. For five minutes they struggle as Super-Wayne flails around the pitch uncontrollably, unable to get the air past his dicky knee. Finally the crew gives up and rolls him back up.

If Wayne's demise is not sufficient encouragement, North Melbourne—first side out—can't break through its own crepe paper banner. A logjam of players develops as the crepe proves too tough an opponent. If this represents the thrust of the Roos attack, Sydney would surely prevail. We laugh as Farnsey and friends belt out 'Waltzing Matilda'.

They say the roar of a full MCG at ball-up can bring a man undone. The roar is all encompassing, there is no place to hide, you are there, in the middle of the G. As the thirty-six combatants prepare for the bounce, the 93,000 fans let it rip, a deafening blast of excitement and expectation.

The roar does not faze Sydney. Big Greg Stafford, a long way from Wagner Oval, wins the first tap and the Swans are off. Luff, Kelly and Hueskes get early touches, each beating their North Melbourne opponents to the ball. Then it's Shannon Grant in possession after a ball up near the Swans' 50. In one movement he grabs the ball and kicks it into the pocket, seconds before he's flattened by a cheap, late shoulder charge. High up in the Great Southern Stand we conquer our vertigo, rising as one as the umpire awards a free kick where the ball lands—just 25 metres out from goal at about 45 degrees. Plugger steps up for his first kick of the game; total focus amidst the cheers and jeers. He strikes the ball deliberately as we lean forward to plot its progress through the big posts, all those miles down. After two minutes, Sydney leads by a goal.

North Melbourne replies swiftly. First Wayne Carey, the Roos' skipper whose all-round skills coupled, with his chivalrous attitude towards the opposite sex (embodied in the celebrated line 'your tits are too small', which earned him a fine and a week of headlines) make him one of the AFL's most recognisable faces, kicks a point after a spell in Sydney territory. Then Dunkley misfires with a clearing kick, straight to North's half-back line. They send the ball back downfield and big Darren Crocker marks 25 metres out over the top of Andrew Dunkley. It's the beginning of a long afternoon for 'Jerry', the tension from the week-long citing circus manifesting itself physically. The rock of the Sydney defence vomits on the field and in the rooms during half-time. Crocker goals truly, giving the blue-and-white face-painters their first decent cheer of the day.

Ten minutes in and thirty-six players all strive to make their mark on the game; pushing that bit harder, giving that bit extra to get into space. It's the unfashionable Sydney players, the second-rungers who are putting their hands up. First, Troy Luff, twice rejected now treasured by the Swans, bursts down the left wing, toeing the ball to within 30 metres. Then Stafford wins possession in defence, firing the ball to Wade Chapman who roosts the ball 60 metres downfield where Mooney and Cresswell are waiting with two Roos defenders. Three attack the ball, the other Cresswell's head; Sydney gets another free within kicking range. Again Cresswell shows how much his kicking has improved through the season and Sydney is up by five.

The play has a manic pitch to it; the combatants throwing their bodies, their fists, their boots, into their work. The crowd feeds on the frenzied activity which, in turn, heightens the hysteria. Some of the cheap shots lead to goals, others go unnoticed. Wayne Schwass throws punches at Luff, who is starting to exert his superiority up front. Then Roo defender David King slides in feet-first at Craig O'Brien's face.

In the post mortems this moment would be remembered as pivotal; the Swans' second focus of attack effectively knocked out of the match. The Swans are in attack at the edge of their goal square; Paul Kelly in space sees O'Brien lead and chips a 15 metre floater. O'Brien surges but the ball is marginally short. As it rolls clear, King slides at O'Brien then collides, connecting first with the toe of his boot then the shin. The initial impact splits O'Brien's face open, requiring fourteen stitches to close; the second cracks the cheekbone. Plugger's old St Kilda team-mate is helped from the field, his face ballooning like the elephant man. While he will force himself to return late in the game, his contribution for the day is over. As O'Brien lies prone, Dunkley cops a boot in the face upfield. Allison breaks clear to kick Norths' second goal and even up the scores.

The advantage swings like a pendulum. Stuart Maxfield makes one of his distinctive breaks on the wing, sprinting 35 metres down the left before centring the ball to Troy Luff. Luff gets his hands to the ball, before Schwass gives Sydney its trifecta of kickable frees by coming over the top late. The North Melbourne fan sitting next to me, the only soul in a thousand block of Sydney fans, curses. Luff coolly converts from 40 metres and Sydney is back in front. The pendulum swings back: it's Allison again, scrambling along the boundary line and grubbering a soft goal. And back again: Dyson bursts out of the centre, feeding Maxfield. Again the blond flier zeroes in on Luffy, this time he marks cleanly over the top of Schwass. 'Luff is in the air!' we screech the familiar cry as he goals with a sweet strike from 45 metres out, 45 degrees around.

It's five minutes to quarter time and a Swans roll is beginning as extra men appear near the ball. The Swans' two most experienced players, Kelly and Bayes, combine to find Jason Mooney at the top of the 50; seeing red and white jumpers everywhere, he drills to Luff, who finds Bayes running around the Roos' back pocket. The last Roo defender charges him and he floats a short handpass to an unmarked Lockett who thumps the ball through from point blank range. The sequence has been crisp and assured, each move executed like clockwork as the North defenders flounder. 'We can win this,' Juzzo screams at me. I'd never really contemplated that, I'd wiped even the possibility out of my mind. Now it was looming.

Dyson and Cresswell again take possession midfield, the ball runs loose and last week's hero, Dale Lewis, ambles in to lob the ball soccer-style towards goal. Lockett and Kickett compete with the Roos' two backmen. The ball goes loose and Plugger swoops, fending off all Kangaroos and Swans in his path. Finding a metre of space, he hoiks the ball over his right shoulder and it wobbles through the sticks. Another point to Cresswell on the siren takes Sydney to a three goal lead and we're singing the Swans' song buoyantly.

In the break we are buzzing, invigorated by the surges of euphoria around each Swans goal. It's more intense than anything—natural or synthetic—that I've experienced. Sydney is leading a grand final, looking in control and ready to sheet the advantage home. Across the aisle the Roo fans are pasty white under their face paint.

From the restart North attacks. Shannon Grant, the youngest player on the field, fumbles in front of his own goal, but recovers and clears the ball to O'Loughlin, who has been securing vital possessions across the half-back line all afternoon. The Swans sweep downfield, running away from the Southern Stand. Bayes to Stafford, out to a flying Cresswell on the wing who sends the ball into attack. Roos defender Fairley has the box seat, but Mooney uses his strength to bump him out and grab the ball in the gap between the half-forward and full-forward lines. Mooney swoops and drills the ball through from 40 metres. Juzzo weeps as we go to a four goal lead.

The danger signs of a blow-out are there for North; you get the feeling Sydney only needs to kick another goal to start running away with the game. Kelly gallops onto the ball and shoots from 50 metres, even though he could have run further. The ball sprays off his boot and misses. O'Loughlin gains possession midfield and Luff and Cresswell both miss marking chances. Luff wins a ball-up inside 50 metres and passes to Kelly, again with time to spare. He sees Plugger free, a 5 metre zone in front of him—place the ball there and the big man will swallow it. The ball drops 50 centimetres short, a half metre that Rodney Eade would later argue cost Sydney the game. Of all the Swans it is Kelly, the inspirational skipper, the man who never gives up, who misses two of three chances Sydney has to really exert its superiority.

So instead of Lockett shooting for a five goal lead, North gets possession and sweeps back down the field towards Carey. Dunkley is on him and smothers the ball but it bounces loose towards Glen Freeborn who snaps a goal calmly. Sydney heads drop, the five goal buffer is down to three. Methodically, North Melbourne works its way back into the game. If there is a change it's around the Roos half-back line; they start winning good ball and surging downfield. The Swans half-back line of Paul Roos and Adam Hueskes, which has dominated for the first thirty minutes, begins to feel the pressure. Freeborn snaps his second goal from another Carey deflection and North Melbourne is back to within three.

Sydney fights back as both sides exchange behinds, the intensity of the contest building as the margin narrows. Lockett looms in the 50: lunging but missing a mark under heavy double-teaming from Martyn and McKernan; then kicking a point after a Stafford lead. But the Swans keep coming, Plugger finally kicking his fourth after a length of the field movement involving Dyson, Stafford, Chapman, Garlick, O'Loughlin and Maxfield, who bursts through the half-forward line to find Lockett in the goal square. Seventeen points up and we're smiling again.

But this is as good as it will get. In a brutal final two minutes of the quarter, North Melbourne piles on three goals and a point to go two up at half-time. Crocker, Allison and Freeborn stamp the Swans' Premiership dream into the MCG turf; snapping clean, clinical goals as the Swans look on helplessly. All three goals are the result of superior scrambling, the Roos now outnumbering Sydney near the ball. McKernan, now on Stafford, is winning in the air, as the Swans attack breaks down at the vital, final pass. The two teams go to the long break with the Swans fans ashen-faced; 19 points in ninety seconds has knocked the stuffing out of them. Across the aisle the face-painters are starting to sing as my hangover returns in spades.

Third quarter, it's North Melbourne by two, but scores can be deceiving. The Roos are winning the 50–50 possessions now, pressuring the desperate Swans. For their part, the Sydneysiders appear deflated, shellshocked that their comfortable lead has been whittled away. In the 1995 rugby union World Cup, New Zealand claimed they were drugged before the final; Juzzo begins to hatch similar conspiracy theories as the leaden-foot Swans struggle into the second half. North peppers the goals, kicking five straight behinds. Sydney is still within seven, but it could easily be 30. Then the Roos start kicking straight, Scholl marking in front of the posts.

Lockett pulls it back to eight points with his fifth goal, marking a Stuart Maxfield kick at full-length like a cricketer in the gully, but Scholl replies in kind after a North Melbourne free. Sydney keeps fighting, remembering all those games throughout the year when they'd clawed their way back from big deficits.

Andrew Dunkley, the man who had repeatedly shown that focus in the tight matches, runs at an innocuous kick across goals. It's a regulation mark for Dunkley, no other players around, but he opts to punch it instead. For the first time all season, the sick and stressed Dunkley, who carried more pressure than any other in the lead-up to the game, misses the ball completely. It floats over his head, bounces at a 90 degree angle and trickles across the goal-line. North by 22. The bloke next to me is up in his seat, cheering boisterously, but the Swans are silent.

Another Darren Crocker goal, a snap from a bounce in the goal square, adds to the pressure; the lead is now 27 points. Three minutes from three-quarter time and we need a goal desperately. The Bloods are still throwing everything at North but there's a desperation that has not been seen all year. It's like they know the match has turned and something special is needed. The irony is that all year they escaped from these situations by doing the simple things well; now in the face of their biggest challenge they go for the miracle play. From the restart Maxfield breaks, shoots and misses from 60 metres on the run, despite having acres of free ground in front of him. Seconds later

O'Loughlin marks from Maxfield inside 50, keeps running, but steers the ball wide for a point. Then it's Roos storming into attack but kicking the ball out on the full. Finally, Kickett marks on the siren and winds up for a big torpedo. But the player who dazzled Sydney with his long-range goals all season has looked lost out there today and leaves the ball short.

A pall of depression envelops the Swans supporters as the North fans celebrate. Games can be won and lost on maybes and we have many to ponder. But the reality is that North Melbourne has been converting its opportunities while Sydney has merely been going close. For me, the final quarter is a blear of frustration and unrealised hope. The lingering memories are the mistakes by Hueskes and McPherson, tiring members of the defensive line who had worked relentlessly under fire all day. Both pick out North Melbourne players within kicking range to field their worst kicks of the season, leading directly to goals that add to the final blow-out.

But the Swans keep going—when a game is lost, there is nothing else to do. Lockett kicks his sixth; O'Loughlin finally snaps one accurately and it's back to four goals. Any glimmer of hope is snuffed out within seconds by Carey, who centres to the appropriately named Rock. He goals and it's all over. Even Derek Kickett's last ever goal can't ease the pain. The blow-out everyone was predicting has even-tuated—we just didn't see it coming.

When the final siren sounds it's North Melbourne by 43 points. The blue and whites stand with arms aloft as the Swans wander around in a daze. The media later talk of the tears and dejection in the Sydney rooms as the enormity of the moment confronted them. I can't talk for them, hell, I just watched them, but from where I sat the hard part was that we were in it; not that we were beaten, but that we could have won. In the back of the Southern Stand we rise to our feet, not knowing whether to clap or cry, just wanting to silence the North Melbourne song. We have come a long, long way, but we fell at the final hurdle.

Weaving down the ramps of the Great Southern Stand, that irritating North Melbourne ditty ringing in my ears ('Good old North Melbourne, da da da da da dum'), I again experience that oh-so-familiar loser's feeling. But the pain does not cut as deep as those North Sydney semi-final losses of my other life. Then we were denied even the contest; the Swans could never be accused of that.

The Swans had given me a grand final, something I knew the Bears would now never deliver. They had led us to the top of the mountain and shown us the view. We may not have made it to the land of milk and honey this time but we knew there was a passage there. They say teams have to lose a grand final before they can win one—1996 had been preparation for that future victory.

That night we drink half-heartedly in St Kilda, still agape at Melbourne at grand final time. Kangaroo fans roam the streets, still in their blue and white war paint, revelling in their victory. It had come in a year when they put their identity on the line, offering to merge with Fitzroy to secure their long-term future, only to be rejected by the Lions. Who could begrudge them their moment when they had walked the tightrope to extinction?

For their part, the Southerners were very nice about Sydney's loss; far warmer to us in defeat than they would have been if the Swans had succeeded. The threat to Victoria's supremacy had dissipated for now and they were happy to drink with us.

I start thinking about what it meant to be a Swans fan; to put up one's hand and say 'I'm part of Sydney'. Sydney; the city the rest of Australia views as crass and shallow, a victim of its history, scale and superficial beauty. The Swannies had shown another side; the unfashionable battlers who no-one expects to succeed, like the teeming masses who live out of view from the harbour foreshore, who endure life under the flight path, sacrificing affordable homes for the thrill of hosting the Olympics. People who are beaten around the head by Sydney but still embrace it as home.

The Swans had helped Sydney flip its perspective. The big fish was the underdog and, for once, we liked the feeling. We showed humility by embracing the unknown. We exposed ourselves to ridicule from those who knew the game better. We fell in love with Plugger, Kelly and Roooos and cheered the courage of their mates. The exhilarating ride to the MCG had drawn us together as a city, giving us something to cheer for en masse. I realised then that we had lost nothing.

Meanwhile, at the SFS

Anthony Sharwood

The 1996 ARL grand final was like a scaled-down version of rugby league's year. Fierce storms lashed Phillip Cox's woeful non-weatherproof stadium just before the main game and returned again after full time. The goings-on between the two storms lacked punch in comparison.

In the stands the huge St George army outnumbered the Manly fans. Led by 'Skull' the Saints were at their obnoxious best, although the noise didn't overshadow the fact there were thousands of empty seats in the members' section.

The match itself was a pedestrian affair with conservatism, rather than brilliance, the order of the day. Manly dominated through its sliding defence and St George seemed to have lost its confidence, afraid to try the speculating kicks which had broken up the defence of more fancied rivals en route to the Big One. Neither team dared to set the match alight, preferring the predictable and oh-so-boring strategy of five hit-ups followed by a kick on the sixth tackle.

The negative play kept the fans well and truly out of the action. The crowd noise in between the brief flare-ups of exciting play was almost non-existent. There were several periods of play lasting ten minutes or more where the crowd barely moved, apart from the odd shuffle of boredom in the seats. In essence, the problem was that there was no competition for possession.

In the end, the outclassed St George team was ground down by a two-'Man' assault—the well-drilled Manly team and the referee David Manson, whose 'not held' decision allowing Ridge a try just before half-time appeared an even worse call than the seventh-tackle 'try' of the 1995 grand final. It was yet another occasion when the referee's performance was the main talking point after an important rugby league match.

The post-match speeches were directed at empty blue seats with the St George contingent already on the trains back to Kogarah and the rain starting to fall again. Rugby league got one thing right compared to the AFL though, the losers were at least accorded some recognition with their captain invited to speak. But when the aging, soon-to-be-dethroned monarch, King Arko launched into his standard spiel about a magnificent exhibition of the greatest game of all, it was clear he still thought the Sydney Swans were the inhabitants of the duckpond in nearby Centennial Park.

After the
Siren

Full-time

Three days later, thousands of Sydneysiders cram Martin Place for a civic reception. Bob Carr vows never-ending support, predicting the Swans will fly 'onwards to victory' while Lord Mayor Frank Sartor, the one who looked like a lost kid in a candy store when he took the flag at the Atlanta Olympics closing ceremony, screeches out 'Go the Swannies' in his falsetto.

Banks of television cameras hone in as the players, looking surprisingly respectable after Mad Monday in blue shirts and ties, are individually introduced to the crowd. The biggest cheers are reserved for the big four: Plugger and Kelly (both sporting Mad Monday crewcuts rather than the traditional Mullet), Dunkley and Roooos.

Sober-looking businessmen and pensioners sporting red and white beanies stand side by side with wide-eyed schoolgirls. Again, it is the cross-section of followers that is most striking, a snapshot of Sydney. As the players leave the stage we fire up for one more rendition of the Swans' song, the tune we so wanted to sing on grand final night, the song that had rung out across the SCG so often in 1996.

'Cheer cheer the red and the white
Honour thy name by day and by night,
Lift that noble banner high
Shake down the thunder from the sky.

Whether the odds be great or be small,
Swans go in and win over all
While her loyal sons go marching
Onwards to victory'

As I threaded my way through the crowd and back to the office, it strikes me that Sydney may have finally gained a soul. The city derided for its crassness, sleaze and lack of substance is celebrating. Not victory, but something much more: the unexpected triumphs and unrewarded efforts of the Sydney Swans' 1996 campaign. After fifteen years being ignored as eccentric triers, also-rans and upstarts, the Swans are part of Sydney.

The Friday after the grand final a Full Bench of the Federal Court gives Super League a comprehensive victory, over-turning Justice Burchett's decision and the ARL's grip on the game. As News Ltd celebrates, ARL clubs scramble for a future. Many consider jumping ship now that the war is over, but Foxtel's commercial opponent in the pay TV war, Optus Vision, quells the defections by injecting another $100 million into the ARL competition. Money, and the division it inevitably causes, wins the day again.

And so rugby league is given the worst result imaginable. Two competitions in 1997 with the only certainty being that neither will be as strong or commercially attractive as a unified one. For News Ltd, defeat in victory. The whole premise of their 'vision' had revolved around cranking rugby league into a 'super' game, played on a grand scale, with the world cheering from the sidelines. What they ended up with is a second-rate conglomeration of yesterday's superstars and tomorrow's nonentities. Beneath the glossy window-dressing, the silly headlines predicting ET will become a world star, is the reality that half the clubs would be made up of nobodies.

Over the coming months the two organisations would release their separate draws for the 1997 season, ensuring a fragmented code. Having come so far, neither could compromise now that they'd sold their soul to corporations who were playing a much bigger game. Having pocketed the huge pay cheques, many of the players naively call for peace, unaware that it was their own avarice that had helped place their game on this irreversible course.

The reality that rugby league must face in the late 1990s as it postures to take on the world is that it has become a business. First News Ltd wanted to take the ARL, an organisation made of and for the various clubs, onto a corporate footing. In its efforts to resist this challenge, the ARL surrendered itself to News Ltd's corporate competitors. The result is the same. League is now a business.

And like all businesses, League must now perform to survive. It has chosen to sever its community roots and will live or die on the largesse of businessmen. The real fear for any League fans that remain is what will happen if the business becomes unviable? Will News Ltd and/or Optus Vision just decide to wind the game up, divest it of assets, like other under-performing enterprises? With other sports like rugby union and AFL thriving, the commercial decision could be made to do away with this idiosyncratic game. And how will it be remembered? As a victim of the pay TV war or a monster that gagged on its own hype?

A week later, the second issue of *Footyzine* is launched with a kick around at Camperdown Park. The Swans diehards all rock along, sizzling sausages and swapping stories of grand final night in Melbourne. Few are coherent but most involve beer, nightclubs and the intervention of bouncers—although these were typically motivated by pity rather than aggression. None of us mentions the result, only the great atmosphere of grand final day.

We are invited to take part in four quarters and I strip down for my first real game of Aussie Rules at the age of thirty years and sixteen days. After coming so far this season, it seems an appropriate, if not reckless, way to end my odyssey. As the motley crew straggles onto the field I join the other fat bastards on the forward line, a tacit group consensus that the fit guys will play on the ball. It's shirts versus skins, about twenty per side, with enthusiasm taking precedence way above skill.

Ball up and the tall guys fly, the opposing ruckman looking ominously accomplished. The ball dribbles 5 metres and a dozen hands dive on it. We all cry 'Ball'. There is little of the fluid attacking sequences that we all came to admire from the Swans. More often than not another League convert grabs the ball, tucks it under his arm and goes for a run, getting caught before you can say 'Pass it, you lunatic'. Then the ball is upon me and I grope at thin air as it goes rolling by. For an irresistible second I think I'm going to scoop it up on the run, but this is not the SCG and I'm not Derek Kickett.

The few blokes who come from Victoria begin to shine, kicking goals for either side as the mass of self-appointed rovers marshal the ball from one end of the field to the other. The difficulty I have is anticipating where it's going to go; I run to the open spaces but the ball goes the other way, I stay in tight and the ball goes wide.

Now I'm caught in the ruck and someone is running at

me, running with purpose, reliving their own Saturday arvo fantasy. My natural instinct is to take him around the ankles, but I remember the AFL rules, waist and shoulder. I take this for the equivalent of the League ball-and-all tackle, commit myself late and hit him with my ever-expanding frame. The guy is stopped in his tracks as the ump calls free. I've made a play! A few of my team-mates clap me and I feel great, I've made my first meaningful contribution.

But better things are to follow after quarter time. Fuelled by snags and VB I see a speculator heading towards me, hanging as usual near the posts. I go high and take a two-handed mark uncontested. I feel like Tony Lockett as I take my mark and walk back deliberately. I feel like Anthony Rocca when the ball sprays wide from point blank range. Now I experience the despair of a missed opportunity, and I look sheepishly for a place to hide.

But I'm tuned into the rhythm now. Grabbing a second mark and picking up a team-mate down near the posts. I try a controlled kick like the ones I practised in the park one weekend, rotating the ball as it hits the foot. Amazingly it floats sweetly to the goal square and is marked and converted. Another touch out of the ruck, this time I snare the bouncing ball and try to handpass it out to the wing. It floats OK but the guy out there misses it. Still, three touches in the quarter and I don't care that we're getting flogged, I'm in the game. That's the sweet thing, being part of it, getting a touch.

Buoyed by a six foot four ruckman who has obviously played before and an average age some five years younger than my team, our opponents spend most of the third quarter scoring cheap goals. I stand up near our 50, chatting with my marker, who is feeling as useless and unwanted as I am. We just can't get a decent kick upfield without losing possession. It doesn't help that only two of our players have shown themselves capable of catching the ball.

Finally a midfielder breaks clear and the ball sweeps (well, bounces really) down the left wing. It's actually closer to soccer. I run towards the goals as desperate Diego Maradonas try to soccer it through. Without warning the ball bounces clear and I'm running with no-one in front of me. I think of just toeing it through, but decide I can't stand the embarrassment of missing another gimme. I grab the ball and boot it from about one metre, but it feels as sweet as a 60 metre game-breaker.

Minutes later, I'm in the play again. Making eye contact with big Snag Cleaver before a ball-up, I run into a gap just in front of the goals. The ball comes to me like clockwork and before I know it, I've dropped it on my foot and it's wobbled about 20 metres for another goal. The defence stares at me in disbelief, but it won't detract from my finest sporting moment in years. They're calling me a 'goal sneak' and I feel just fine.

Two goals to the guy in the batik shirt! It mightn't have looked pretty, but I get a few pats on the back from my team-mates and quizzical gazes from the defenders who can't believe how someone who looks so crook can kick straight.

'Conserve your energy, that's the secret,' I offer free advice as we collapse at three-quarter time. I'll run around like the complete novice I am for the rest of the afternoon but the glow of my little victory will keep me going for days.

Then the game is over and we're lying like casualties on a battle front. The afternoon is still and quiet, but our heads are buzzing. Those who haven't played before, the Converts, are feeling the post-match glow; while the Converters like Eddie and Juzzo smile on as if to say 'we told you so'.

As the sun sets across the city a stillness comes over the park and amidst the beer and bangers we are content. We have found a new sporting passion, tinged with the regret that it's taken this long for us to meet properly. Like any new friend, we're filled with expectation of what the next meeting might bring, in awe at the potential richness that we can bring to each other. We're already counting the days down to the 1997 season.

Who knows what the future will hold for Aussie Rules in Sydney? Perhaps the Swans will go bad, Plugger's knee or groin gives in, Kelly goes to Brisbane, the wins stop coming. Maybe we'll be back to the 4,000 per game of the early 1990s. It might all unravel, but I doubt it.

As people look for a game to celebrate their city and their country, chances are that Aussie Rules with its rich traditions and pragmatic but responsible engagement with the future, will become an integral part of Sydney, something for the city to nurture, to cherish and to enjoy. And in the end the game will be stronger for us. With Sydney a genuine AFL town, the AFL will be a genuinely national game, a game with the weight of history behind it and community bonds strong enough to grow and thrive into the twenty-first century. A game which can unify and define cities as Australia struggles to make sense of its place in a contracting world, providing identity in the benign face of homogeneity.

And even if it doesn't, Sydney will never forget the one year Aussie Rules gave comfort to a city on the rebound, a city whose own game had ditched it and was in desperate need of some distraction. 1996 will always be remembered as the year when the Swans soared high, all the way to the MCG on grand final day, and we, the converts and Swannie-come-latelies, for a moment soared with them.